MW01062372

Reflections in the Rearview Mirror: Lessons in Leadership

Terence F. Moore

New York, NY

ISBN: 978-0-578-02490-5

To Peggy J. Lark,
my assistant for more than three decades.
No professional has done
more to enable me to survive and thrive.

Contents

Prologue

"You haven't been where I have been,
but I have been where you are.
I am not here to hear myself talk.
I am here hoping you will listen.
While I share some observations and advice.
If you don't, I'm wasting my time and yours."

—Tommy Lasorta, talking to a minor league
baseball team in Midland, Michigan
July 2008

Introduction

"When I was a young man
Darned if I didn't know it all.
When I was young like you,
Lord, I knew it all.
But if you listen to this old dog bark,
You may see the holes before you fall."
—Song by Johnny Paycheck

This book is intended to provide wisdom to managers and leaders at every level in the field of business, particularly the business of healthcare administration.

Those best qualified to offer advice are those who have been successful in the field of healthcare administration for an extended period. The contributors who were interviewed for this book are all respected individuals who have had distinguished careers—many of them maintaining a CEO position for approximately thirty years and/or until retirement. Each contributor was selected based not only on long-term career success, but also based on my personal knowledge that each of them has character traits that make them worthy role models for the rest of us. They include Andy Allen, Sandra Bruce, Jerry Fitzgerald, Doug Peters, John Rockwood, Mark Taylor, Sam Wallace, and Gail Warden. Provided in Appendix A is a brief biography for each of these contributors. Most of the interviews were conducted via phone, transcribed, and then approved by the contributors. Key comments were taken from each of these interviews.

A portion of the text came from my thirty-six years of healthcare experience—thirty-one years as a hospital and health system CEO. Previously, in books and articles, I have documented some of my experiences that are referenced throughout this book.   The landscape is littered with executives who have lost their positions—sometimes through no fault of their own, and sometimes because they have violated some of the suggestions contained in this book. There are an even greater number of executives who are stuck in situations where their advancement is halted. It is my hope that this book will serve to reduce the possibility that a manager or healthcare leader will experience job loss or career derailment because of a tactical or strategic error.

It is important to note that the comments and advice included throughout this book are not necessarily that of the individual contributors unless noted as direct quotes from them. There was no attempt to gain contributor consensus on any of the subjects within these chapters. Contributors have only approved comments specifically attributed to them personally.

Lastly, I have borrowed from the literature without reservation. So much good material has been written in recent years on the subjects of leadership and management, as well as physician relationships and board relationships, that any book not drawing heavily from the "deep well of knowledge" outlined in books and articles can only be described as shallow.

An outline of chapter content follows:

Chapter 1 describes some of the background and experiences (often early childhood and college) that contributed to the success of the executives.

Chapter 2 is about those issues executives learned later in their careers that they wish they had known when they began. Wisdom comes with experience. This chapter is about wisdom.

Chapter 3 provides an overview of effectively working with the management team. An executive's success, failure, or even their eventual derailment, depends on their relationship with the rest of the management team.

Chapter 4 is about working with the medical staff. Every medical staff is different, but every physician falls within a certain typology. No hospital or health system can advance without *some* members of its medical staff working cooperatively with administration. However, most every hospital also has physicians who are non-contributors to the organization's advancement.

Chapter 5 addresses working with boards. Board members occupy the most powerful position in any healthcare organization, yet they often know the least about healthcare delivery. Boards can be one of the "keys" to an organization's success, or they can be the reason for its failure. Board members are sometimes under-appreciated, but alternatively, they sometimes are not held as accountable as they should be for an organization's decline or demise.

Chapter 6 describes some of the mistakes executives have made. Some make big mistakes early in their careers, and some make them later in their careers. I have made them throughout my career. This chapter is closely tied to the next chapter.

Chapter 7 is about overcoming failure. How we bounce up off the bottom determines more about our future than how we handle success. If we are to survive, we must use our experiences to empower us, not imprison us.

Chapter 8 describes some suggestions for career survival and success. It is the rare individual who doesn't succeed because of his or her own initiatives. The world is full of brilliant people who have gone nowhere, because they did not do the "right things." This chapter is about the "right" things.

Chapter 9 contains some concluding thoughts about the value of having good character, and some characteristics of successful leaders.

There was a time when healthcare executives enjoyed relative job security compared to their counterparts in private industry. They did not suffer from the ravages of economic recessions or product life cycles or foreign competition. That time ended with managed care, DRG reimbursement, outpatient "skimming" ventures by other providers and investors, and severe cutbacks by third party payors.

Healthcare executives now entering the field are more likely than not to be forced to move at some point during their healthcare careers. If this book enables one executive to survive and thrive in his profession, it will have been worth all the time and effort of those who contributed to it.

Chapter I

What Shaped Us

*"Talk low, walk slow, and always have
some place to go."*
—John Wayne, Actor

Each of the contributors had a strong family background, although their childhoods were very different. Some grew up in a rural environment, some in an urban environment. All had mentors who helped them become who they are. Indeed, mentors, and as a minimum, a support group, is essential for anyone to maximize her potential. Sandy Bruce said:

"I came from a family-oriented family, where my parents' values obviously instilled in me a strong sense of responsibility for each other and for others less fortunate. My family tended to take in other children; families that needed help always seemed to be a part of our family. I think this had a significant impact in my approach to healthcare both to employees and to the core mission of what healthcare is all about, which is really trying to improve the status of people. I think it has made me an activist. I had a father who never really accepted a complaint about a situation unless you brought with it a solution, and I think that has also made me competitive. I grew up in a family of all boys and I was the youngest girl and treated equally by my father. My brothers didn't necessarily treat me with any respect, so I think I learned early on how to win my way through all kinds of worlds that included, obviously, men and women."

Jerry Fitzgerald had an interesting background, and states:

"In my case, I think that I was certainly not a standout academically until I got to graduate school. Academically I chugged along. Certainly, being at parochial school up until graduate school afforded me a discipline that applied to real life. It develops some of the habits of follow-up, investigation, inquiry, and the need for continual learning, which all came about from that educational environment, and those things transfer to real life. I think that the single event or process that allowed me to succeed both academically in graduate school as well as in real life were my experiences as an All-American fencer in college. I was captain of our fencing term. I was invited to go to the '64 Olympic trials—finished, I think, eighth in the country. I still teach it, but it certainly gave me a snapshot of overcoming failure. Actually, having the ability to be that successful in that sport, even though I had played football and track in high school, my success in fencing with my coach caused me to become an all-A student my last year in college and to do extremely well in graduate school. I believe it was the ability to be successful, manage my time, and manage what it really, really takes to succeed. In that particular sport, I found how I was applying myself in high school and college academically, but I had to apply myself in terms of effort to succeed to the level I did in fencing. It certainly opened my eyes to what capacity we all have that we don't use, and then when I did use it, what one could achieve. You learn that if you have had the opportunity to experience a situation through massive effort, you can achieve great things."

Fitzgerald goes on to say:

"I wanted to be an automotive engineer and started out in the engineering school, and my desire has always been in automobiles and racing. I think if I were to do one thing over again, I would not have skipped out of my Olympic training camp for the 1964 Olympics. I believe I would have gone on to be an Olympic champion, or close to it, but I skipped out because I thought I was pretty good and didn't need to stay at the training camp. So, I ended up in the last round after winning for two days and ran out of gas, because I wasn't physically prepared.

In terms of starting over, I wish I would have had the ability to excel at something earlier. I probably had those opportunities, but didn't apply myself, because I didn't know any better. So it would have been great if I could have had a coach like I had in college. I had coaches, but they weren't like my college coach."

Sam Wallace recounts that:

"From a background standpoint, I would say that surely my dad, who was Secretary of the school administration and superintendent of the schools of a small school district in Missouri, had a big influence. He died a couple of years ago, and I continue to look back and see things that he said and that did influence me. I didn't exactly know I was being influenced at the time, but later on you look back and say *that* had some way of influencing me one way or the other. I certainly think that I grew up in a place that didn't have a lot of sports and things, so I became really involved in Boy Scouts and still am—forty-some years later. I think that going up through the ranks and being on the board and now being on the national group has provided a lot of leadership training. That's just the way they do things. I have been around Scoutmasters and good leaders throughout, and kind of emulated what they did—and I guess the third and final influence is in the military. I went through ROTC at the University of Missouri and was in the military for three years—in Viet Nam for the last year. It had a big impact on me with regard to background and leadership and understanding what direction I should be going with a career, because before that I really didn't have a clear direction."

Gail Warden, who ran major healthcare systems in some of the most metropolitan cities in the United States, grew up on a farm. He said:

"My family background is probably the thing that affected me the most—the work ethic and values that I learned from my father. I grew up on a farm in Iowa, and from the time I was five or six years old, I was up at 4:00 in the morning and out there doing chores with my dad, taking responsibility, and I would say this had an influence on me as I grew up. My dad had terrific values and that had a real impact on my view of the world. Basically his values were what you'd expect from an Iowa farmer —working hard, being willing to always have integrity, help your neighbor, do unto others as you would expect them to do unto you, etcetera. All of those are things that are important as you go through your career and you learn how those values count. I think as I reflect upon my career that there were two or three events in my life that probably had the most impact. One was when we moved from Iowa to Colorado because my little brother (who was then a baby) had really bad asthma and would not have been able to survive if we stayed in Iowa. Basically, we had to pull up roots. I had only gone to a one-room schoolhouse until I was in the seventh grade, and then we moved to Colorado. There was only one other person in my class—JoAnn Harland—and she was very smart and pushed the hell out of me all the time.

When I was young, I hated her because she was always trying to outdo me. And as it turns out, she was probably one of the best things that ever happened to me. Moving from that kind of an environment to one in which I ended up in a big consolidated school system was a big change. I rode a bus for about an hour and twenty minutes every day to school from out in the boondocks of Colorado. That was the first thing that had an impact on me, I guess. The second was the decision I made to go away to school, which was a decision that did not set well with my father, yet at the same time I think it was probably one of the smartest things I ever did—go out East to school. I got a good scholarship; I worked two jobs. I received an education that I probably wouldn't have gotten if I had stayed home and gone to school in Iowa or Colorado.

The third major event that was (and still is) a tremendous influence was the influence Walt McNerney had upon me. I learned a lot from him, and one of the things that I will never forget is when he called me in his office one day. He said to me: 'You have great potential, but you are not going to take advantage of it unless you put your mind to it, because things are too easy for you.' He said, 'I expect you to do things that nobody else has ever done.' That was a pretty big challenge to have somebody put before you. But as it turned out, he and I have been really close friends for all these years, and he is somebody that I relied upon for mentoring and input."

Doug Peters focused on what he learned in school versus

what he learned in life and indicated that both are important. He said:

"One of the intriguing things is the difference between what we all learned in school and what we have experienced in real life. There is a big difference. Hopefully, what we learn in school is that hard work pays off. You can't just skate, and that is a lesson. There were many theories in school that are often different from what we experience. The variety of subjects we learned are just faded memories for me, but the idea of having to buckle down, meet deadlines, commit to schedules and so on—that was a lesson learned in school. Life's experiences teach us that experiences are more visible (memorable). So, while I cannot recall some of the things from college or graduate school, I believe we have all derived good and bad from experiences in our work life. I have learned that any executive who takes himself or herself too seriously has lost some perspective about where real leadership fits in the schedule of things. Lastly, having a sense of humor is important and it should be appropriate—not inappropriate."

Like most of the other contributors listed at the back of the book, John Rockwood didn't start out wanting to be a healthcare CEO. He said:

"I was the oldest in a family of five, and I think the oldest tends to learn pretty quickly that they are in charge. I think that experience of being the eldest was helpful. The other experience I had that made a big difference occurred in 1965 when I got out of undergraduate school. I didn't know what to do, but I knew I was going to get drafted, because that was in the midst of the Viet Nam War, so I decided to go to officer's candidate school and came out a Navy Ensign. Then I ended up spending a year in Viet Nam on the Saigon River where we supported the Marines. We operated a number of small boats that went up the Saigon River. I was twenty-two years old, and you get put in these situations where you have forty to fifty people reporting to you, and the one thing you learn pretty quickly is that you don't know anything. And the people that work for you are mostly people without my level of higher education, but they have a lot more real-life experience and know a lot more than you do about their jobs. So, I think you get an appreciation for the value of other people in understanding, knowing what you don't know, and being able to rely on others to help you with work and decisions that must be made."

Mark Taylor said, "I have been very lucky in my career in that I have had two or three people who I can truly look back on and say they were mentors. None of them were formal mentor relationships. I do not believe there was ever a moment where the individual sat down with me and said, 'I think you have some good things going. I am going to really spend time working with you.' It was just the opportunity to watch and learn from these people—and some of them were just the off-handed comment someone might make. For example, someone once told me that it is not about talking a good game—you have to bring home the 'bacon.' It was a moment where I could see in my own experiences I was busy trying to move a number of different things at the same time and realized this is not about how many things you can get done, it is about making sure that the high priorities get done. There are moments like that where I can look back at what those individuals said and just the opportunity to watch them work through an experience."

A number of us were strongly influenced by our military experiences. John Rockwood was an ensign in the Navy and spent a year in Viet Nam. Sam Wallace was an Army officer and also served in Viet Nam for a year. I was an Army officer and paratrooper who spent much of my time training troops in the use of chemical munitions.

The leadership lesson many of us learned in the military is summarized in a 1999 *Harvard Business Review* article. Jason Santamaria, who served as a Lieutenant in the Marines, described the leadership lesson he learned. "Ian Smith taught me the importance of developing others. He often placed his busy schedule on hold to teach young enlisted Marines about the Corps' history and traditions, as well as the leadership principles and values. Finally, First Sergeant Smith taught me a lesson I will always carry with me: that leaders inspire people by demonstrating a genuine concern for their welfare. Whenever a Marine faced a personal emergency,

First Sergeant Smith focused his individual attention to the problem until it was resolved. If Marines were temporarily transferred to another unit, he periodically visited them to ensure that their needs were being met. Every time one of the Marines completed a technical school or a leadership course, he attended the graduation ceremony and shared in the accomplishment. His efforts built an intense loyalty to the unit and inspired every one of its members to achieve higher levels of performance."[1]

One of the invaluable lessons I learned from my military experience is that a key to leadership is being out in front. Officers' training, whether it is the Army, Navy, Air Force, Marine, or Coast Guard, forces their cadets to be out in front of others. It is not about seeking the limelight or taking credit for the work of others. It is a willingness, and even an eagerness, to be in front of others, whether it is chairing a meeting, giving a speech, or providing leadership on a work detail.

When we were in Alabama during one phase of our training, all of us had the same shaved-head haircuts, same olive drab uniforms; we all looked alike. Each day the cadre would pick someone out of the ranks to be a platoon leader, company commander, or some other leadership position. It didn't make much difference whether the person was a superior soldier or just average. At the end of the day, you began to believe that the person out in front was the leader. More importantly, the person who was out in front started to believe he was the leader, and became better at leading. If you have not experienced this phenomenon, it may seem to be a fictitious observation, but it is as true in civilian life as it is in the military.

There are two reasons why people don't lead. If you don't lead it is for one of these two reasons or both. The first reason is that many people do not want to invest the time its takes to lead. It takes a lot of time; many nights and weekends of working while many others are playing or just passing the time.

The second reason is that people are afraid; they allow their fears to control them. Anyone who states they are never afraid is either lying or a fool. As the late Katherine Graham, publisher of the *Washington Post*, said, "Courage is not the absence of fear—it is the ability to act in its presence."

One of my heroes, the late Col. David Hackworth, who, at one time, was the most highly decorated soldier in the U.S. Army, said, "Bravery is being the only one who knows you are afraid."

The lesson is: never, ever let your fears control you. Don't be reckless or foolish, but never fail to act, simply because of fear. The CEO contributors, to a person, all have faced challenges on an annual basis that required courage and enormous commitments in time and energy. The very fact they have all lasted so long at the top of their profession is testimony to their tenacity and courage.

Chapter II

If I Knew Then
What I Know Now

*"If I had known I was going to live this
long, I would have taken better care of myself."*
—The late Cary Grant, actor

Hindsight is 20/20, and wisdom comes with age. Those statements may be clichés, but they are true, nonetheless, and they directly pertain to the subject of this chapter. The comments in this chapter are responses to what the contributors and others wish they had known early in their careers.

Administrative Assistants

There are some things I may have known early in my career, but I never fully appreciated their importance until decades later. One such issue is the importance of administrative assistants and secretaries. As Keith Ferrazzi states in his book, Never *Eat Alone and other Secrets of Success, One Relationship at a Time,* "Make the gatekeeper an ally rather than an adversary. In addition, never, ever get on his or her bad side. Many executive assistants are their boss's minority partners. Don't think of them as "secretaries" or as "assistants." In fact, they are associates and lifelines."[1]

These individuals occupy a position that is much higher in the organization than their titles suggest. A "truth" is that their power/influence is directly proportional to the length of time they have been associated with their immediate superior. If there is a secretary who has been working with her boss for five years or more, one can be assured she is communicating with her boss about people/problems, etcetera. in the organization on almost a daily basis. And, you can be certain her boss listens and hears most of what they are saying. If it is about you, and the comments are not favorable, you have a problem.

Treat these people like gold. Get to know them. Remember their birthdays. Do something for them. And, once you get to know them, listen when they tell you something, or make a suggestion of any kind.

Sam Wallace said he wishes he had known that being blunt was probably the best policy, even though he said he didn't feel he was blunt enough throughout his career. I know him, and I would say he is very "tactfully blunt." He said, "Telling people exactly where they stand is not earth-shaking, but something I wish I had done more. I have had to let eight people go in the last five years, and one always thinks of those as personal failures. In your mind, you can recall telling them this or that, but I always wonder if I was direct and blunt enough about it."

It may be true that being blunt with subordinates is the best policy, but it certainly is with superiors as well. When dealing with superiors (especially if you are relatively new to an organization) be brief, be blunt, and be gone. Too many young executives don't seem to know when to leave or when to listen. Some even want to get into a debating contest.

Jerry Fitzgerald said he believes the ability to be more aggressive with the expression of your own opinions about what you can do for a community, and also the practice of taking insights from other work environments as you go through your career is important. He believes that he spent twenty to thirty years being too focused on healthcare, even though the opportunity to be engaged in other unrelated businesses would have made him a better decision maker and would have given him better insights into problem solving.

Sam Palmisano, chairman and CEO of IBM, provides some sage advice. He states: "Some of the best advice I ever received was unspoken. Over the course of my IBM career, I've observed many CEOs, heads of state, and others in positions of great authority. I've noticed that some of the most effective leaders don't make themselves the center of attention.

They are respectful. They listen. This is an appealing personal quality, but it's also an effective leadership attribute. Their self-lessness makes the people around them comfortable. People open up, speak up, and contribute. They give those leaders their very best."[2]

John Rockwood said that thirty years ago he wasn't aware that life is simpler than most people think. He said,

"When I meet people, they look at me and think, you have a very complicated job and you must be so bright and all of that." He went on to say, "It is a tough job, but you don't have to be a rocket scientist to be in this industry. I remember going through school and looking at kids who were getting straight A's when I was getting B+'s or B's in undergraduate school, and thinking that they would be the ones who were going to be the most successful. Intelligence has a role (you can't be an idiot), but there is a quality which is a lot more important than pure intelligence. I believe it is the ability to see clearly what you want to have happen and to be able to think those things through conceptually and to trust people. If you cannot do those things—you can be the brightest person in the world, but you aren't going to get anything done. From that, I think the one thing I have learned is don't be afraid of additional responsibilities. The job is complex if you let it be, but you can make it a lot simpler if you want to. Nothing is impossible if you apply yourself."

I asked another executive from outside the field of health-care what he wished he had known early in his career. His name is Frank Popoff, former president and CEO of The Dow Chemical Company, which employs approximately 48,000 people. Popoff said he wished he had listened more. He also discussed what he termed "target blindness." "Target blindness" comes from a phenomenon that originated in the military when a dive-bomber pilot was so focused on the target (often the smokestack of an enemy ship) that he failed to pull up his dive at the right time. In management, it occurs when someone is so focused on a goal or objective that they compromise the organization or division for which they are responsible. The need to listen more and talk less was a theme of many of the CEOs interviewed and will be discussed in other chapters.

Popoff also said he wished he had understood what he terms "gravity." Gravity, according to his definition, is the reality that what goes up must come down. It is true of product life cycles, the stock market, and other areas of business. In other words, just because things are going well, doesn't mean that will continue, and just because things are not going well does not mean they won't improve at some point.

Turnarounds

Most of the contributors have been involved in turn-arounds, and those who haven't, have been through one or more downsizings. Some of us have written books about it.[3] This subject is so important to most healthcare executives that it is worth learning what advice an expert in this field recommends.

Regarding all that he has learned about turning around bankrupt companies, which he does for a living, Alfred J. Moran, Jr., CEO of Gerant Companies, Inc., states that "It doesn't matter what business you are in. I have found that the same five steps apply every time. I wish someone had told me this twenty-five years ago instead of having to learn it the hard way. Here they are:

Step One: Grab the cash. Most companies in trouble are also hemorrhaging. Cut deals with vendors. Sell assets. Stop payments. Do whatever you need to do to corral the liquid assets immediately. Do not delegate this function until it is well in hand. Until you have done this, you are not in control.

Step Two: Freeze the expenses. Don't worry about revenue for now. Just lock down the expenses. Cut everything you can, including executive salaries. Let them feel the crisis and share in the solutions.

Step Three. Interview everyone you can. All the information about what is wrong and what should be done is already in-house.

Step Four: Formulate a strategy for the direction of the company. You are better off with a half-right strategy now, than a perfectly right strategy in six months. By then, it will be too late.

Step Five: Draw up the "ideal" organization chart to reflect the minimum necessary staff to implement the strategy. When you do this, start fresh. Ignore the people who now work for the company. After you have the ideal organization chart, go back and slot in the people you have if they fit somewhere. Most managers take the existing staff and try to find a job for them. This is disaster. Lay out the organization first. If people don't fit, get rid of them. Sounds cold, but executives are paid to execute.

That's it. Works every time."[4]

Annie Fisher, a columnist for *Fortune* magazine, had some worthwhile insights when addressing the question, "What is the one piece of advice you wish you had been given?" She contacted hundreds of people regarding that question, and some of the better responses are as follows:

- Have friends at work, but don't get caught up in it. Being supportive after hours is fine, but spending too much time in the office or the company cafeteria helping that borderline personality who has boss problems will ultimately reflect on you. Once that teary friend is gone, you'll be remembered as her or his supporter, and the "evil boss" will doubt your loyalty.

- Dress for the job you want, not necessarily the one you have. That way, when your big chance comes, it isn't difficult for people to see you as someone to be taken seriously. It is unfortunate that appearances have so much power over perception, but that is reality.

- Study successful people—in your life, in books, in your company—figure out how they got where they are, including what choices they made and what obstacles they overcame. A lot of people have come from nowhere to accomplish great things, and if they can do it, you can too.

- If it doesn't feel right, don't do it. Ethical decline often begins with 'just this once'—and when you are down that slope, it is a very slippery climb back up.[5]

With regard to the last recommendation, one thing I have learned is that the "character" of those you contract with is critical to the success of not only the relationship, but also of the business or venture. It may be difficult to discern, but if you know the other parties have a history of questionable moral and/or ethical behavior, it isn't worth your time and energy to do business with them.

Use of Legitimate Power

Something I may have known early in my career was the responsibility of legitimate power, but those responsibilities have broadened and become crystal clear to me over the past three decades.

Legitimate power is sometimes called the power of the prince, or organizational power.[6] It is the power that comes from holding a particular position. It is fickle and will be gone the day you leave your position, but while you have legitimate power, remember it shouldn't be misused. Its use should be as follows:

- It is not about having others serve you. It is about being of service to others.
- It is not about self-praise and stories about yourself. It is about listening more and probing others about their thoughts, observations, and recommendations.
- It is not about golf courses, country clubs, and condos. It is constant communications, contact, and responsiveness to those to whom you report and who report to you.
- It is not about being aloof and above others. It is being available for almost anything at any time and "being there" for others.
- It is not the end of learning. It is the luxury of being given time to learn while earning a living.

- It is not about being surrounded by comfortable offices/surroundings. It is being where the "action" is as much as possible.

- It is not about special parking privileges. It is parking closest to your workplace only if and because you are the first one to arrive at work in the morning.

- It is not about "blamestorming." It is about knowing that, ultimately, responsibility for mistakes and failures of those who work for you are yours.

- It is not about glory for yourself. It is about giving credit and glory to others.

- It is not always about success. It is sometimes about overcoming frailties and failure.

- It is not about being attended to. It is about being attentive.

- It is not about you. It is about others with whom you work.

All of these uses or misuses of organizational power help establish what type of leader you are.

Perhaps one of the best explanations about why power must be used appropriately and consistently by an executive comes from Tom Peters. He states, "I have no sympathy for those who complain of a loss in the last thirty seconds of a game. If they had been ahead 27-7, then a fumble in the last 30 seconds would not have cost them the game.[7] Peters believes that the appropriate use of power is about building up a 27-7 lead. Indeed, it is about doing a lot of things right on a daily basis. And, as Peters says, "The big show-down where slaughter awaits you might have been avoided all along if you hadn't been a jerk." [8]

Chapter III

Working with the Management Team

"We are all angels with only one wing.
We can only fly while embracing each other."
—Warren Bennis, Ph.D.

One of the better books about managing people—people at every level —is "The Hands-Off Manager".[1] The authors state that all managers have two communication styles from which to choose: 1) Hands-on: They criticize and judge their people; 2) Hands-off: They mentor and coach their people.

They emphasize that far too many managers spend their time criticizing, correcting, and controlling. The authors state that, "Real power in leadership comes from partnering, not criticizing."[2] Hands-off managers commit to finding how their people can fit rather than fixing people who don't fit.

The relationship of the CEO to his or her management

team is key to not only the organization's performance, but to the CEO's own sustainability as well. Indeed, in a book I co-edited about hospital turnarounds, we learned that the importance of the CEO's relationship with the management team cannot be overemphasized. Management teams are built on similar values, compatible expectations, and mutual respect.[3] Gabarro states that "Perhaps the most salient difference between the successful and failed transitions was the quality of the new manager's working relationships at the first year.[4] Every attempt must be made to cultivate an effective working relationship among members of the management team.

One other phenomenon has become apparent to me in recent years, regarding how a CEO relates to his or her managers. It is particularly true of new CEOs in a turnaround situation but often happens even when the organization is not in a turnaround situation. In failed turnarounds, the CEO fires several managers soon after arriving (which is also true of successful turnarounds). The differences with a failing CEO or supervisor occur when they begin to fire some of the people they have hired after twelve to twenty-four months. Others (particularly the board members) then begin to understand what the problem is. The CEO then becomes a bullseye for the medical staff, board, and others. His or her position is eventually "overrun." If you see a CEO or manager who is in the process of terminating many of the managers he or she hired, the chances are great that the manager or CEO's tenure will be short.

The CEO of a medium-sized hospital terminated most of his direct reports within six months of his arrival. He even bragged about his efforts to "clean house" as he termed it. Within eighteen months of hiring their replacements, he began firing the people he had hired. Within twenty-four months, the board had a special executive session and terminated the CEO (to the cheering of the employees).

John Rockwood led an effective management team for years, and states:

"There is a lot to process, but a definite process will not get you anywhere unless you can achieve what you want to achieve, and I believe one of my frustrations in dealing with people is that there is a very logical way to get somewhere, but it is too long and cumbersome. There is probably a right way to do it in a perfect world, but we don't live in a perfect world. I believe that people like us are judged by what we produce— by what we get done. We are not judged by how we do it. It doesn't mean that the end justifies the means. All it means is that you can get too hung up in these processes and forget why you are on the road. We have some really bright people who work here. But some fall short in two areas. One type are those who really want to go through each step and want to make certain that all the right people are there and there is a way to do something and there is really only one way to do it. Then there are other people who are maybe at the other end of the spectrum and just want to get something done and they don't care how they do it. I am not saying that one should ignore the process, but I believe my job is to produce results, and frankly, nobody cares about how we get there. There must be some sort of urgency to produce results."

Rockwood is also a believer in consistency and "up-front" dealings with the management team and others. He said:

"Being consistent and having others understand your values is important. I would rather get the news out (good or bad) instead of thinking about when we should tell people, because I believe most people in the CEO position are going to want to do the right thing. You want to trust them with important duties, but you should also want to trust them with information as soon as you have it that is going to affect them. Straight communication is part of what we do. It goes back to ethics, but may just be one's view toward people, the goodness of people, and the fact that they can accept bad information just as they can receive good information."

Gail Warden states that:

"If you want to build a strong workforce and sustain a good culture, you need to expose every employee to the same experience and regular reinforcement. We had a renewal program here, which turned out to be very successful and resulted in a whole new mission, vision and values. It also got people focused on the idea that our real business is taking care of each patient first, and that patient has their own special needs, and that it is our job no matter where we work to identify that. Employees need to be rewarded through recognition, family events, and personal attention on the part of management.

You have to create a vision for them, which they can buy into and understand, and you must keep it simple. You cannot make it too complex. And, when you are setting priorities, it is much better to set two or three priorities that everyone can understand and espouse, than to have twenty priorities and then confuse them."

Mark Taylor believes that a management team is not formed by good luck or just the selection of good people. He states,

"The selection of people is important, but you need to have focus—you need to have some method for personal development. Formally write out what your management philosophy is—how do you want this group to work together? What it will look like when it is successful? Having laid that out, focus specific training and experiences to help the management team develop on those areas.

Another component is to not hesitate to evaluate your group's performance against what you set out as a leadership philosophy. We have what we call "leader promises" here. They are posted in every work area and department at least on an annual basis. Some managers ask their employees to grade them. When the staff does that, it gives the manager a sense of where they can do better. A high performing management team isn't created by good intentions and great wishes, nor is it just an education process. It is focused training and timely feedback about improving yourself as a leadership group."

A common theme among several of the executives interviewed was the need to take action sooner rather than later when a member of the management team needs to be removed. Doug Peters said:

"The single failure that comes to mind is not removing a destructive person in a group of excellent staff. The person was actually competitive, but had inconsistent values with the rest of the team. I tolerated that and tried to work with him. It didn't work, and it went on too long affecting the rest of our group. The lesson is—don't wait. People are generally at a point in their career where they apparently cannot change their values in an underlying way. If they can't, and it doesn't fit what you are trying to accomplish, you have got to take action to remove that person rather than taking the long, long road to trying to change that person while you are losing the rest of the group."

Gail Warden made a similar comment. He talked about a man who had a great influence on him. The man was Jim Campbell who was initially chairman of medicine and then president of Rush Presbyterian in Chicago after the medical school and hospital were merged. Gail said, "Probably the biggest lesson I learned from him was that if you have a gut feel about someone (that they are not going to deliver), deal with it, and deal with it quickly. Do not think you can rehabilitate him or her, because you probably cannot. Don't try to be a hero, and do not think that just because nobody else has been able to turn the person around that you can."

Sam Wallace oversaw twenty-three hospitals in Iowa and described the evolution of their core management team. He said:

"Our core management team was made up of all the administrators, plus the corporate VP, and others. The group got together once per month and went out for dinner in addition to their formal meeting. There was an attempt to give every administrator one thing to do for the whole system. Some worked at it more than others, but it gave them a chance to work with others throughout the system.

Initially, the group thought they might vote on key issues, but it isn't a democracy —it is an advisory group. The decision, after all input is obtained, is made by the CEO.

Collectively, we tried a lot of thing over the years—best practices, etcetera. Many initiatives worked well, but some didn't. Since we didn't want to merge with all the small hospitals in the state, but we wanted them to know we would work with them in certain areas, it was my idea to hire a guy to put together a whole department to do that. He even bought a pick-up truck, which you are going to relate to small-town Iowa. He went out to those hospitals and said 'We are here to help you.' They said 'Get to hell out of town.' It didn't work, and we don't have that department anymore."

Some believe that employees fall into the "20/60/20 principle."[5] The top 20 percent are the cream of the crop, do their job, have integrity, and work hard whether their boss is around or not.

The middle 60 percent are people who are pretty good at their jobs, do what they are supposed to do. They're not great, but they are good.

The bottom 20 percent are the exact opposite of the top 20percent. They are worthless to both the organization and to your customers. They do not achieve results.

Andy Andrews emphasizes the importance of being direct and honest with not only the management team, but with the employees as well. He said:

"We had 350 employees and, like many organizations, we used to have employee meetings, which I always enjoyed doing. I think it keeps you intellectually honest, because here you are dealing one day with a surgeon who is making a million bucks and in the next five minutes, you are working with environmental service workers who were making somewhat above minimum wage, and both are realities. That is one of the things I liked about healthcare, and that is that you are dealing with a whole cross section of the community. I think it not only keeps you intellectually honest, but hopefully a little humble about what your responsibility is to them and their families. You have a responsibility to them and management can cause harm to peoples' lives that can just be devastating. I had 350 people in an auditorium, and I was explaining to the employees that we had done data comparisons about contributions to employee health benefits of .our competitor, which was the Western Reserve Care System. I should note that their nurses were unionized and their LPN's salary was a fixed percentage of what their RN's salary was. So it kept coming up and, frankly, the licensure in Ohio doesn't allow the LPNs to do very much. They can't start IV's, etcetera, so it wasn't practical or cost effective. We simply couldn't afford some of the practices of our competitors (one of which is now close to bankruptcy).

I am in this room with 350 employees—one of the men got up and said, 'I'm a pharmacist. You just told me I'm going to pay more for my health insurance, and you're telling me I'm not getting a pay increase. That doesn't make me happy, and if I'm not happy, how can you expect me to provide good service to the patients of our hospital?' It lit my fuse. So, I went into a tirade. I said, 'I'm going to tell you something. My wife works at a bank downtown. She's a branch manager. She has employees that have worked there fifteen years who are making a little bit more than minimum wage, and they haven't had a wage increase since they started there. They pay $100 a month for parking because they are downtown. When they find out that she's married to me and I work at St.

Elizabeth Hospital, they ask her how they can get a job there because it's the best place in town to work. I am going to continue to make this the best place in town to work, but we also have fiscal realities here.' I got a standing ovation. Shooting straight is something I have had to learn over time, whether it's dealing with physicians or whoever."

The top managerial team, for the most part, is at the top 20 percent. They wouldn't have/shouldn't have gotten to where they are, unless they were in the top 20 percent. Larry Winget states, "You manage them by staying out of their way. Find what they need to do their job. They need your encouragement and support, and don't need you looking over their shoulder."[6]

As for the middle 60 percent, that is where most managers need to spend their time. The leader's job is to move people in this large middle group into the other two categories.

The other category that has not been mentioned is the bottom 20 percent. Write them off, save your time, get rid of them in a professional way. By doing so, there is an opportunity for those in the 60 percent category to move into the bottom, but until you get rid of the people who were already there, there never was any room for them.[7]

In looking at the history of our own organization, many managers have been there for decades, but there seems to be a turnover of about 15 to 20 percent of the managers on a yearly basis. These are managers who didn't fit or didn't perform. In most cases, we did the right thing and worked with them to find positions elsewhere. Many of them have had long and successful careers in smaller organizations. As with most organizations, the turnover rate of managers who have been there one or two years appears to be higher than those who have been in the health system for five years or more.

In working with their administrative teams, CEOs and senior managers would do well to heed the advice of Ronald Heifetz, the professor of leadership at Harvard. Heifetz states:

Most leaders die with their mouths open. Leaders must know how to listen. The art of listening is more subtle than most people think it is. But first, and just as important, leaders must want to listen. Good listening is fueled by curiosity and empathy: What's really happening here? Can I put myself in someone else's shoes? It is hard to be a listener if you aren't interested in people.

Some of the best-known leaders are in a dynamic listening mode, asking questions all the time—not getting seduced into trying to provide all of the answers. If you're the boss, the people around will invariably sit back and wait for you to speak. They will create a vacuum of silence and you will feel a compelling need to fill it. You need to have a special discipline not to fill that vacuum.[8]

Summary Comments

It is impossible to describe working with the management team without mentioning the elements of leadership that influence the leader's relationship with other members of the team. Warren Bennis suggests that there are four competencies that determine the success of a leader in today's markeplace:[9]

1. They understand and practice of the power of appreciation. He believes most organizations are woefully negligent in bestowing either acknowledgement or appreciation.
2. They keep reminding people of what's important. He believes we are all hungry to find meaning and purpose in our work and contribute something beyond ourselves.
3. They generate and sustain trust. Bennis notes that 25 percent of the American workforce has been laid off at least once between 1985 and 1999—and that number has surely risen in today's economy. Trust is a combination of competence, consistency, caring, fairness, candor, and authenticity.
4. Lastly, and most importantly, for those who lead others, the leader and the led are intimate allies.

Bennis reminds us that great leaders are made by great groups and by organizations that create the social architecture of respect and dignity.

The bottom line is that employees will not treat patients any better than they treat each other. They will not treat each other any better than they are treated by their manager. Their managers will often mirror the behavior of the CEO. Therefore, if the CEO and top management are dissatisfied with patient satisfaction surveys, they should first look in the mirror.

Chapter IV

Working with Physicians

> *"I'm the recess playground supervisor."*
> *—A physician in a small hospital, talking*
> *about his role as chief of the medical staff.*

In their relationship with the medical staff, administrators run the gamut from being subservient to ignoring the physicians almost completely. Several years ago, I had a conversation with a fellow administrator who took obvious satisfaction in the fact that he only had one physician on his hospital's board—and that physician was selected by the board and not by the medical staff. In the next sentence that same administrator was bemoaning the fact that none of his medical staff took the time to meet with the Joint Commission on the Accreditation of Hospitals during their recent survey, and consequently, the hospital was placed on a provisional status.

This situation illustrates the results of ignoring the medical staff or attempting to keep them out of the decision-making process. Healthcare executives must be advocates of involving members of the medical staff in organizational affairs—particularly within the hospital's formal committee structure.

The need for physicians and administrators to work collaboratively has never been greater. Over the past few decades, physicians have begun to be the biggest competitors to many hospitals. At the same time, there are more salaried physicians than ever before, and managed care (especially PPOs and PHOs) has forced senior administrators and physicians to work together in ways that were largely unknown in many parts of the country several decades ago.

In two of our system's smaller hospitals, there were no salaried physicians fifteen years ago. Today, more than 80 percent of the physicians and physician extenders in those two hospitals are salaried.

Physicians, particularly in states where there is no Certificate Of Need (CON) legislation, have taken a large portion of the outpatient market that once was dominated by the hospitals in the region. Physicians operate surgery centers, MRI centers, CAT scanners, laboratories, rehab services, and a number of other profit-making ancillary services.

A friend in Indiana (a state that does not have CON legislation) said "In one week, we lost 85 percent of our ambulatory surgery volume when a group of orthopedic surgeons, gastroenterologists, and ENT surgeons opened their own ambulatory surgery center near the hospitals."[1]

Statements about the innate conflicts that will always exist between administrators and physicians are nonsense and only serve as an excuse for a "do-nothing" approach. Conflicts between the two *are not inevitable*. The only inevitability is that some physicians and administrators will never "get along," but that should not deter efforts to involve representatives of the medical staff in strategic as well as tactical decisions.

There are sufficient studies indicating that most (or at least many) physicians have a negative view of administrators, and this attitude is certain to influence physician behavior. The results of a survey of fifty physicians and fifty administrators by P.K. Associates, Inc. of Madison, Wisconsin reflected the unfortunate perception each group often has of the other. "The majority of physician respondents characterized hospital administrators as being aloof, insecure, autocratic bureaucrats who were too much concerned with finances and too little concerned with patient care." A Missouri internist, for example, said, "Our administrator—like all administrators I have worked with—is more of a cost accountant than a person. He is devoid of passion." Conversely, a majority of the administrators who were interviewed characterized physicians as egotistical bumblers who were unable to organize their own lives or records and who were constantly rebelling against the better-organized administrators.[2]

As might be expected, the study of the fifty administrators and fifty physicians found that in every instance where good physician-administrator relationships were reported, the responder also indicated that there were open channels of communication between the two groups. Furthermore, cooperation was greatest in small hospitals (where the administrator interacted with all the doctors), and in physician-owned facilities (where the profit motive greased the wheels of communication).[3]

Another study that was done as a Ph.D. dissertation involved ten hospitals and the perceptions of their CEOs and their counterpart physicians regarding issues leading to the formation and destruction of cooperation.[4]

Honesty/dishonesty

Honesty was the single most important factor either positively or negatively influencing the amount of cooperation between physicians and administrators. This treasured commodity between management pairs is not easily acquired and maintained, primarily because the individuals must be totally—even painfully—open with each other. At the same time, they must survive conflicting pressures that not only threaten the individuals, but their cohesion as management pairs. Robert Kaplan's work on openness (the foundation of trust) between people offers little hope for optimal cooperation in the hospital environment with its conflicting dynamics. He states that "Openness can occur between two or more individuals when: a) There is a high level of collective commitment and interpersonal closeness which is associated with limited and minimal hierarchy, and b) By institutionalization, or the deliberate effort to secure the willing adoption of atypical social practices." He adds that "Openness is inappropriate and virtually useless in disintegrative, competitive, and politicized situations."[5]

Healthcare organizations are well known for their fragmentation, competition, and politics, which occur both internally and among hospitals in the same region. Competition is a fact of hospital life, and as the stakes get higher, so does the level of institutional competition. Physicians and administrators must now begin to cooperate more vigorously within their institutions if they hope to survive the increasingly competitive pressures placed on them by the outside environment. If one looks again at the list of barriers to cooperation, man could be eliminated if there were greater trust in the relationships.

Table IV-1, shows those traits that produce cooperation by each of the parties involved in the study—administrators and physicians. Table IV-2 shows factors inhibiting cooperation by both groups. Note that in both tables the factors are ranked as to their importance. For example, "honesty and trust" was the most important trait administrators can have to promote cooperation from physicians and "displaying a respect for me," was considered the least important trait administrators can have for promoting physician cooperation.

Table IV-1: Most Significant Factors Promoting Cooperation		Table IV-2: Most Significant Factors Inhibiting Cooperation	
Administrators' Traits Producing Physician Cooperation	Physicians' Traits Producing Administrator Cooperation	Administrators' Traits Destroying Physician Cooperation	Physicians' Traits Destroying Cooperation
1. Honesty/trust 2. Intelligence 3. Enthusiasm/ energy/hard worker 4. Knowledge of job 5. Compatibility 6. Willingness to take a position and offer a solution 7. Attentiveness 8. Loyalty 9. Mutual respect 10. Display of respect for me	1. Honesty/trust 2. Enthusiasm/ energy/hard worker 3. Intelligence 4. Knowledge of job 5. Compatibility 6. Listening 7. Willingness to take a position and offer a solution 8. Modesty 9. Willingness to compromise 10. Friendliness	1. Lack of initiative/ Enthusiasm 2. Incompetence 3. Dishonesty 4. Heavy bias in performance 5. Taking adversarial position 6. Lack of native intelligence 7. Wastes my time 8. Divided loyalties 9. Lack of education	1. Dishonesty 2. Incompetence 3. Lack of initiative/ enthusiasm 4. Lack of personal friendliness 5. Refusal to listen 6. Arbitrary decisions 7. Manipulation 8. No follow through 9. Failure to maintain a confidence

Tom DeFauw, president of Port Huron Hospital in Michigan, and someone I had the privilege of working with when he was the president of the Gratiot Medical Center in Alma, Michigan, emphasized that, "A strong relationship with the medical staff is the foundation of success." He further stated, "One may sometimes take unpopular positions with the medical staff, but it is important to be honest, consistent, and communicate frequently with them."

Methods to include M.D.s

Joseph Bujak, M.D., one of the most respected authorities and speakers about the best methods to effect collaboration between physicians and board/administration, believes strongly in what he terms "dynamic facilitation" to resolve issues. His suggestion is to contract with a professional facilitator whose job is to listen and foster open/safe communication.

He suggests using four flip charts. On the first, he suggests writing down the issues the group believes are important. The second chart is the "What should we do about it" chart. (Anyone who suggests an issue for the first chart must also suggest a solution). The third chart is about the perceived incompleteness of the previously suggested solutions. The fourth chart is "extra stuff" that doesn't merit being on the first or second chart. With the right facilitator, Dr. Bujak says it works almost every time.[6]

The appropriate amount of physician involvement varies from one situation to another. Some methods of involving physicians in organizational decisions are:

1. Appoint physicians to the board and to various subcommittees of the board. Don't give them token responsibilities or ask them to serve without voting privileges.

2. See that administration and even the board are invited to attend some of the medical staff

committee meetings. It is particularly important that the CEO or alternate attend meetings of the executive committee of the medical staff.

3. Appoint special task forces, such as a building expansion task force, to effectively integrate physicians into projects.

4. Develop a matrix organizational structure that facilitates the input of physicians, particularly where physicians are responsible for a geographical area or clinical service.

None of these means is a substitute for informal communications—which should be open and often between the administration and medical staff.

Richard Thompson states that most physicians are not gung ho organization people and suggests the following caveats when working with physicians:[7]

1. Don't set impossible goals. Do not expect all or even the majority of physicians to participate in a particular survey, process, etcetera.

2. Don't equate lack of interest in organizational matters with professional incompetence—there is probably no correlation between the two.

3. Don't expect organizational initiatives from physicians. However, physicians are important "sounding

boards" for organizational change.

4. Don't overlook professional and personal relation-
    ships that may not follow organizational lines. It
    would be difficult to overemphasize the impor-
    tance of informal alliances between physicians and
    administrators. In our experience, the most effective
    working relationship between the administrative
    and medical staffs occurs where there is considerable
    informal dialogue. Successful cooperative efforts are
    a proper blend of efficient, formal organization and
    informal personal and professional relationships. It
    is an error to depend on either one alone.

Even though physicians may be given the opportunity to
be involved in decision making, positive results will be difficult to achieve if the wrong physicians are participating.

Years ago, a friend of mine and I developed a matrix that
can be used in selecting effective medical staff leadership.[8] In
this model, all physicians are evaluated based on the traits
of "attitude" and "action" and are identified by this "style of
rule" exercise involving their personality types.

"Effectiveness," for our purpose, is the ability of the
respective medical staff leader to communicate the interests
and concerns of the medical staff to the board and administration, and to ensure that decisions are made in the best
interest of high-quality patient care.

Drifter/passive mumblers could just as well be called "isolationists." They complain, usually to their close personal friends or others in the community, that the "sky is falling" or "everything is getting worse." They are almost always negative toward any progressive action that is not in some way self-serving. Their negative mumblings are usually restricted to private conversations, and therefore, they are easier to tolerate than some other types.

Dependent/bureaucrats have a positive outlook on life, but fail to act. We refer to them as bureaucrats because they actually find comfort in an organizational setting, especially one in which decisions can be deferred to someone else or made by a group. They can be identified by such comments as, "We are lucky to have things the way they are,'" "Have a nice day," and "I really like …" Seldom do you hear them make an action-oriented statement like, "Let's move on this project."

The worst personality type to appoint to a medical staff leadership position is the **disrupter/vitriolic physician**. Unfortunately, because he or she is often so visible, that person is sometimes elected to a position of responsibility. Too late, it is often realized that these personality types do not represent any concerns other than their own vested interests. Even those who are truly concerned about the quality of patient care may have little concern for others in the organization. These physicians may be descendants of the cowboys in "Old

West" movies who rode into saloons—without bothering to dismount—and fired guns into the ceiling.

The high action, positive-oriented physician that we label the **developer/benevolent autocrat** can wield tremendous influence at the board level and with administration. This person's actions are well thought out. He or she has usually taken the time to analyze any potential counter arguments. I have never known a healthcare organization that advanced without this type of high action, positive-oriented physicians. They are community treasures. Treat them like gold.

Personality Type Matrix and Physician Style of Rule

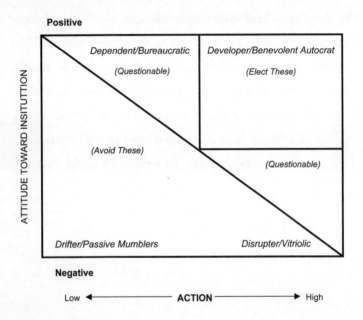

One of the CEOs interviewed, Sandra Bruce, has been especially aggressive in working with the medical staff.

She states, "I created a physician advisory council—it is outside of the mainstream of the medical staff. It has no power other than they advise me, and it has been one of the most effective mechanisms for input and feedback from key physician leaders that I have ever done. It is standing room only. We meet once a month. We meet for an hour-and-a-half, and it always goes to two hours. It is just amazing. We have a medical staff of six hundred physicians, and these are some of the best in the United States. Many physicians choose to come to Boise because of the lifestyle. For them to take the time to do this every month is amazing, but I think it is because we are listening. We change direction as a result of what we are told. They know not to come if they are not going to be honest, bold, and forthright. This is my testing lab for, "Am I on the right track or not?" It has been very exciting.

Another thing we have done is what I call our "Top One Hundred Physician Visit Program." I do one-on-one dialogues with the top one hundred physicians, and by top one hundred, I strictly go by revenue base. I have no idea whether it is profitable, but the top one hundred revenue producers get a one-on-one with me, and I simply have three points that I make:

1. Thank you very much for supporting us.
2. What are we doing well that you would like us to do more of that really makes your heart sing?"
3. What is it that we can improve on that if I fix would encourage you even more to be loyal and more supportive of the institution?

I have found those very effective. Obviously, you have to

act on the information, but it is powerful when the CEO sits down with those doctors on a one-on-one basis. I have also found that if I go to the bottom hundred, that is powerful too. Sometimes I think I should spend more free time there, because if I fix significant problems, I know I move the loyalty agenda. That has been fun, and obviously, I think all CEOs know how critical it is to have physicians on board. My philosophy is that you must partner with the medical staff. I just have a fear that not-for-profit healthcare as we know it will be a thing of the past unless we, as healthcare leaders, find ways to partner with our respective medical staffs, and that goes to the heart of my philosophy statement—and that includes, where appropriate, business joint ventures. We have several of them here, and they are very, very successful."

Physician involvement in a hospital's decision-making process is essential if a generally harmonious atmosphere is to exist and bickering is to be minimized. The effectiveness of physician input not only depends on the quantity of physicians' involvement, but also on the attitude and actions of those physicians who represent the other members of the medical staff.

No chapter about physicians would be complete without some mention of disruptive physicians, the bane of many hospital employees.

As Jeff Goldsmith (one of the best healthcare writers of our time) reminds us, "Like lifelong bachelors contemplating marriage in their fifties, many physicians have little experience with sharing, compromise, or delegation of responsibility."[9]

The Credentialing Institute, which is a partnership between Geely Associates Ltd. and the Horty, Springer and Mattern law firm, have sought to address this issue.[10] They believe that, "For too long, disruptive physicians (which are a small minority of physicians) have been allowed to harass and intimidate nurses, be abusive to patients and their families, disrupt meetings, threaten to sue their chiefs, credentials committee members, and other physician leaders if they review the physician's charts, and generally disrupt the hospital. Why? Because no one wants or knows how to deal with them."

Key to controlling these "bad boys" is the medical staff leadership. Without their leadership and support, progress in sanctioning disruptive physicians is painfully slow or nonexistent. They state that the first step is a clear board policy about disruptive behavior. Secondly, there must also be clear language in the medical staff bylaws about not condoning physicians who do not work harmoniously with others in the healthcare institution.

Thirdly, a detailed step-by-step procedure to investigate complaints. This third initiative must include: a) documentation of disruptive conduct, b) follow up meetings with the offending physician, and c) disciplinary action pursuant to medical staff bylaws.

These policies and procedures are only as effective as those who enforce them. It is ultimately the CEO's duty to not only have the proper policies and procedures in place, but to assure they are executed.

Summary Comments

Some summary "truths" regarding working with physicians:

- Don't ever refer to physicians as "my physicians" or "my docs." ("Your" docs may just be the seed of your demise).

- Your relationship with physicians is partially a function of how often they are in contact with you. Your physical presence can be worth more than written communications or phone calls.

- If an issue has a direct effect on physicians, it outweighs an issue that doesn't. For example, changing from silverware to plastic table utensils in the physicians' dining room trumps some multimillion-dollar mistake because of an accounting system failure.

- There will always be at least 20 percent of the medical staff who don't want to "take the trip" wherever the organization is going. It may be the recruitment of badly needed specialists, the construction of professional office buildings, affiliation with another organization, a major building project, or any of a number of other issues important to the organization's survival.

- Involve the right physicians on the board and board committees.

- The organization will succeed and thrive in spite of some physicians—not because of them.

- Abusive, disruptive physicians are dinosaurs of another time, and no matter how much revenue they generate for the organization, they are not worth having on the staff. It is the CEO's duty to sanction those disruptive physicians in concert with the medical staff leadership. Joseph Bujak, M.D. would argue it is chiefly the medical staff executive committee's role to handle disruptive physician issues—not the CEO.

- Healthcare executives are expendable—the medical staff is not.

Chapter V

Optimizing Boards and Board Relationships

"Having been a hospital CEO and now a hospital board member, I compare it to being a parent or a grandparent. Boards are like grandparents—they don't have the day in and day out responsibilities of parents."
—David Reece
Retired hospital CEO

The first "truth" administrators must understand about boards is that they work "for" them—not "with" them. As one CEO said, "On any given day, if 51 percent of our board members believe I should be fired, I am road kill." Board members should be shown deference at all times. Equally important is an understanding by board members that they have essentially three very important roles.

The board's role is to make an organization:

1) bigger

2) better

3) richer.

Their role is not to manage the organization.

In a survey of several top healthcare CEOs in the early 1990s, they had several recommendations for working with boards as follows[1]:

Probe your board members. To board members, perception is reality. You cannot know how board members perceive the organization's operations unless you ask. A formal board questionnaire should be complemented by frequent one-on-one conversations with all board members. Be sure that you ask what additional information they would like. Do not ask, "How am I performing?" Such a question is self-serving and does not encourage a discussion of issues. At the end of every monthly report, use a sentence that says: "If you have questions or suggestions regarding any aspect of our operations, please let us know."

Show your board you are listening. Follow up on requests for information in writing and within a 24-hour period. When a CEO or other senior executive is fired, a frequent board comment is they did not follow up on suggestions and questions. You show you are listening by prompt follow-up.

Include your board's priorities among your priorities.

If a board member places a high priority on some aspect of the organization's operations or the marketplace, then that issue(s) should become a high priority of the administrative staff. It may be of little importance to the overall operation or effectiveness of the organization; nonetheless, it should be made a high priority of the administrative staff.

One of the medical centers in our healthcare system operated a hospitality home for patient families and outpatients. It represented less than one-hundredth of one percent of our total gross revenues, but it was of great interest to several of our board members. Do you think it was a priority in our reporting? You can bet we reported its activities to the board with some frequency.

Know the board members like a book. You should know everything you possibly can about your board members—who their friends and heroes are, their management styles, and most of all, their expectations. Each board member has different interests and talents; the CEO must take the time to know them in some depth if he is to work effectively with each member.

Work with the entire board. Do not make the mistake of working closely with only the chairman. The strength of the board/CEO relationship is usually the sum of relationships between the CEO and all board members. It is all too common to find a CEO concentrating time and effort in working with the board chairman over time. When the chairman retires or steps down, the CEO has no "power base" and his or her position is "overrun."

The wise executive establishes a broad power base and does it as soon as possible. It requires relentless effort and a plan to communicate effectively and often with everyone a leader wishes to have as part of his support network.

An administrator worked for the same board chair for fourteen years. The chair was a man of influence in the community and handled all of the hospital's communications with outside foundations, as well as with many others of influence in the community. The chair eventually decided to retire from the board, and the new chair fired the CEO within eighteen months. The CEO had not cultivated strong relationships with all the other board members nor with the most powerful people in the community.

Vice presidents and other managers would do well to not only develop a support base within their respective organization, but outside their organization as well. The probability that your immediate superior will be the sole factor in your long-term success is pretty slim. See Chapter VIII for other suggested activities.

There should be general agreement between the board and administration about organizational goals. Goals must be clear, well presented, thoroughly discussed, and agreed upon by the board. If the board wishes to modify the goals or general recommendations of the administrative staff, administration must be sensitive to the board's opinion. It is "career suicide" to deliberately or unwittingly follow a course not approved by the board.

Go beyond the normal board/CEO reporting relationships in working with board members. Do whatever you can to make board members' lives easier. "Friends" may be too strong a term, but make every attempt to have the best possible relationship with each of them. It is a mistake not to socialize with them when invited to do so.

A very successful CEO who was fired from his previous position and spent nine months in an outplacement cubical said he learned that you must never assume board members know and appreciate your work. You must spend a lot of time with them both formally and informally. The CEO learned that important lesson well, and is presently making several million dollars per year in salary and bonuses.

Develop a positive, can-do attitude. Board members like executives who "think they can" rather than those who appear to have a "defeatist" attitude or are indecisive. John Witt, author of *Making Better Boards*, tells of two executives interviewing for a CEO position in a hospital. One was a relatively young physician, the other a seasoned administrator.

The physician, when asked if he could turn the organization around said, "Sure, no question about it." The administrator said, "I do not know for sure, but I will try." The physician got the job. According to Witt, "The physician exuded confidence, because he knew that, depending on which direction he pointed his car when he awoke on any given morning, he could make $170,000/year." That helped foster his "can-do" mentality.

Have key administrative staff members attend board meetings. Some CEOs only allow one or two members of their staff to attend board meetings. These "lone rangers" sometimes run out of "silver bullets" when they come under attack by the board and would be much better served by adequate administrative back up. Rotating members of the administrative team through board meetings is good exposure for them and recognition of their value to the organization. It is also an opportunity to present administrative or medical guests with a token of the board's appreciation.

Provide board members with educational opportunities. Have an in-depth orientation program for new board members. Enable and encourage them to attend local, regional, state, and national healthcare meetings. Allow their spouses to accompany them on these trips. Board members are separated from their spouses every time they attend a meeting, and they deserve to take spouses with them to conferences at the hospital's expense.

Give board members recognition. Board members cannot be given too much recognition. Most are not paid for their talent, time, and effort. Board members, not the CEO, should have their pictures in many of the promotional materials produced by the organization. They should be included and introduced at employee award banquets and other hospital-wide functions. Do not wait until they retire to recognize them and the contributions they make.

Have a progression philosophy and policy to groom potential board members. Hospitals spend tens of thousands of dollars annually to educate trustees, yet often very little attention is paid to "testing" and grooming potential board members. Do this by having potential members serve on standing committees to evaluate them before they are placed on the board. If they demonstrate excellence while serving on a standing committee, then they should be given a position on the board when vacancies become available.

Committee members who are being groomed, but are too busy or apathetic should be derailed. Either remove them from the standing committee, or if that is too awkward, leave them there and remove them within a few years. Often they will leave voluntarily if they are not moved onto the board. In addition, members who are unable to work in a group setting or want to cut costs at any price should also be prevented from coming on the board. The worst type of people who should be "weeded out" before becoming board members are those who have a vested interest that they cannot control.

Board Progression Philosophy

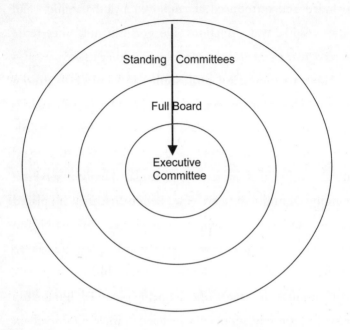

A senior executive from a Fortune 500 committee was placed on a hospital's planning committee to be evaluated as a potential board member. At his second meeting, he stood up and ranted on, using a transparency he had brought, that nurses should not be given any raises until we could compete with the South Koreans (his machine operators were making more than the nurses in question at that time). Needless to say, he never became a board member.

In an organization without a grooming process most CEOs would tell you (in strict confidence) that they would do almost anything to keep 50 percent of their board members and almost anything to get rid of 50 percent of their board members

Avoid frontal attacks. When contentious issues are raised at meetings of the full board, attempt to divert them into appropriate subcommittees or ad hoc task forces. Do not engage in protracted arguments and avoid the urge to "do battle" at full board meetings. All of this is not to imply that board meetings should be "rubber stamps." A compliant board is a dying board, and the clash of ideas is appropriate, but heated confrontations should take place at sub-committees such as the Joint Conference or the Executive Committee— not the full board. Great executives are choreographers. They work behind the second to "choreograph" upcoming meetings—particularly if the agenda items are controversial. To do otherwise can potentially result in what I have heard four different healthcare CEOs say over the years, "I thought we were meeting to discuss my raise and bonus. It soon became apparent that the purpose of the meeting was to demand my resignation."

Gail Warden believes that, "The board is only as good as the CEO and the board leadership wants to make it because it is hard work. You have got to want to have a good board and work at it continuously. You have got to be accountable to them at the same time you have got to make them feel like they have an important role. I told the board I believe the most important committee is the Nominating Committee because that is the committee which decides who the new board members will be and, secondly, the body which is going to provide leadership for the department chairs. If the Nominating Committee does its job, it will get the right people in the right place."

Lastly, Warden says, "You cannot over communicate with your board as good governance takes a lot of time and effective staff support."

Mark Taylor says, "Boards are fascinating—second only to physicians. One needs to admire these individuals who are successful in their own rights in a variety of different careers and endeavors that are willing to volunteer hundreds of hours to the community. Advice I would give new executives who are working with boards is as follows. First, always remember that these people usually come in with very strong skill sets and you should not underestimate them. Bring them in. Have them look over your shoulder. Let them critique you and embrace their critique. Do not try to machine things past them.

Secondly, always remember that while they are skilled, talented people, they 'parachute in' for the board meeting from their own life and career, and will not necessarily have had all of the context of everything that you have experienced since the last board meeting. So always think in this context that you have to keep telling the story, so they do not feel disjointed in the process."

Boards should be supportive of their administrative staffs if they are performing. The first step any healthcare board should take to support and assure that the CEO maximizes his or her potential is to assure the CEO has an employment contract. No CEO should be expected to work in today's healthcare climate without some type of contract with a severance of several years' salary. The greater the tenure and age of the CEO, the larger the severance.

Chief executives can foster better board relations if they occasionally remind themselves that they do not know what their boards are thinking. They may *believe* they know, but unless they continually probe them on an individual and collective basis, they do not.

Establishing and maintaining a board/CEO relationship is hard work, but vital to maximizing both an organization and CEO's potential.

A couple of final thoughts about boards.

Boards often do not receive the credit/blame they deserve for running an organization into the ground. Some board member's aversion to change, cutting costs at any cost, proclivity to "major in minors" and other counterproductive traits cause keep an organization from maximizing its potential.

I received a telephone call one morning from a CEO of a smaller hospital in our region. He asked me to let him know of any job openings in the state. He went on to say he had resigned the previous night. I said, "You didn't quit without having another position, did you?" "Yep," he said. I quit when it was 1:30 a.m. and some of the board members who had insisted on going through every accounts payable check were doing just that and one fell asleep." He was fed up, and rightly so.

There are arguments for and against board members having term limits, but the bottom line (all things considered) is that it is better to have term limits for board members. It is one of the few ways to rid the organization of bad board members. The bylaws should provide for a one-year break in service before the board member is eligible to serve again. Good board members can be brought back on the board. Three consecutive, three-year terms are common for many boards. In our organization, we have board members serving their second and even third 9-year terms after having had a one-year break in service.

One last comment about boards: The irony is that board members occupy the most powerful position in any healthcare organization, yet most know the least about healthcare delivery. A large part of a CEO's survivability depends on how they work for the board and the quality of those selected and groomed for board membership.

Chapter VI

Mistakes Managers Make

"When the gates are all down and the signals are flashing and the whistles are blowing in vain, and you ignore all those facts and lay on the tracks, don't blame the wreck on the train."
—From "The Train Wreck",
A country western song

Having just witnessed a hospital that has had four CEOs in the last 18 months, it is a reminder that administrators as well as boards make mistakes. In this particular situation, it was due more to mistakes the board made than the CEOs. Regardless, all this upheaval at the top has an unsettling effect on the entire organization.

A friend who worked in a hospital owned by a large national proprietary healthcare corporation talked to me about the effect of having a "revolving door" of CEOs. He said, "Every new CEO comes in with a list of things they want to change and their own pet programs. The department heads make as few changes as possible, knowing that the next CEO will want to make other changes—often recommending we do what we had been doing previously."

There are a number of mistakes managers make that can lead to failure or derailment (the term most often used in the following chapter). David Brown best defined a derailed manager as one who, having reached the general manager level, is fired, demoted or reaches a career plateau.[1] These derailed leaders may have a high potential for advancement, impressive track records, and generally been on the "fast track," but they have made some serious mistakes along the way.

Gail Warden states that, "In the fifteen years as CEO of Henry Ford Healthcare System, it has become very clear to me that there are three things that get good people into trouble: 1) not managing their personal finances; 2) a wandering eye; and 3) substance abuse. If you ever stop to think about all the people you have had to fire for cause, it is almost always one of those three reasons."

There are numerous typologies as to why leaders fail, but broadly speaking, they fall into several major categories. There is a lack of vision, lack of team building, communication failure, and/or poor interpersonal skills.

Other authorities provide more detailed listing of issues which cause derailment. Vogl[2] lists the following:

- Suffered from a lack of accountability
- Succumbed to bitterness
- Burned out
- Demonstrated a lack of courage or integrity
- Did not deal with his or her doubts successfully
- Did not handle the expectations placed upon him or her
- Was unable to resolve conflict successfully
- Displayed poor interpersonal skills
- Lacked leadership aptitude or skill
- Had unresolved marriage issues
- Was overly ambitious
- Was filled with pride
- Stopped learning and growing

What makes—or breaks—a top executive? An exhaustive study of executives who had been derailed provides some interesting insights. Reporting the results of this study, Michael M. Lombardo and Morgan W. McCall observed that all of these derailed executives were near the top of a Fortune 500 company, and all had gotten there because they appeared to have the same traits as their successful counterparts.[3]

As these executives rose to higher levels in their organizations, however, certain events tended to expose one or more of their faults. Situations leading to their derailment included one of the following:

1. They lost a boss who had covered for them or compensated for their weaknesses.

2. They were in a job for which they were not prepared (a new boss with a different style was often a factor in exposing their lack of preparation).

3. They left behind a trail of little problems or bruised people. They handled these problems poorly or moved so quickly that they failed to handle them at all.

4. They moved up during a corporate reorganization and were not closely scrutinized until after the reorganization had fully settled.

5. They entered the executive suite where getting along with others under highly stressful conditions was critically important.

What these situations exposed were "people factors" or so-called "personality flaws" in the failed executives. In another study, these same investigators compared twenty-one derailed executives with twenty "arrivers"—those who made it all the way to the top.[4]

Data obtained through interviews with insiders from several Fortune 500 corporations turned up ten "fatal flaws" in the derailed executives:

1. Insensitivity to others—abrasive, intimidating,

       bullying style

2. Cold, aloof, arrogant behavior

3. Betrayal of trust—a comeuppance of others, or a failure to follow through on promises

4. Over ambition—thinking of the next job, playing politics

5. Specific performance problems with the business

6. Over management—inability to delegate or build a team

7. Inability to staff effectively

8. Inability to think strategically

9. Inability to adapt to a boss with a different style

10. Over dependency on an advocate or mentor

Most executives were derailed by only one or two of these ten flaws. Insensitivity to others was cited more frequently than any other flaw. The ability—or inability—to understand other people's points of view represented the most telling differences between those who "arrived" and those who were derailed. Only 25 percent of the derailed managers were described as having a special ability to deal with people; among the arrivers, the figure was 75 percent.

Enough about the failure of business executives in general. Why do *healthcare* executives lose their jobs? For a 1987 article Dr. Earl Simendinger and I wrote, we asked this question of four top executive recruiters in the United States[5]. All four responded that this subject had been foremost in their minds and shared their comments with us in letters.

Mark Silber, a well-known lecturer, consultant, and executive recruiter from San Diego, has given considerable thought to the causes of executive failure within healthcare organizations. He believes that the primary cause is often a miss-match between the executive's style and the organization's culture. This mismatch is revealed in ineffective board relationships as exemplified by noncommunicative, emotional, or manipulative behavior—and even the exploitation of "perks" and benefits by the executive.

The second major reason for failure, according to Silber, falls within the category of managerial skills/relation factors. Indecisiveness or the "paralysis of analysis" is often a characteristic of failing executives who gradually lose touch with objectives, opportunities, and the perceptions others have of their actions.

Their leadership becomes lopsided: they focus on one aspect of managing at the expense of another. For example, they may focus on the visionary aspects of the organization at the expense of bottom-line results. These same executives also fail to network adequately with peers, board members, members of the medical staff, and others.

The third major reason Silber gives for failure is "personal factors." Executives with this problem may project a poor image, be insensitive to power and its use, and exhibit many of the fatal flaws cited in the studies by McCall and Lombardo.

In an unpublished paper, Silber focuses on assistant administrators and their "slow and subtle decline into personal political ineffectiveness." He believes that failing assistants often have the attitude that they are anointed rather than appointed.

Every year in many states, there is a deer-hunting season. Every year, just before the season begins, there are a large number of year-and-a-half old male deer running around, living out in the open, chasing female deer and having a real good time. The first time a high-powered rifle is fired, and they see the deer next to them explode, or a bullet whistles by them, their life is changed forever. They realize they are a hunted animal. The first time an executive is fired or sees others around them fired, they realize none of us are anointed —we are all appointed.

Silber says that often, "These self-styled experts believe their position must be totally accepted and feel frustrated and personally rejected when it is not. They do not know when to listen or when to leave." When dealing with your superiors, be brief, be blunt and be gone.

Mike O'Brian, then president of Harper Associates in Detroit, stated he believes that there is a significant reason why healthcare executives fail—one that has not received enough attention. Assistant administrators learn early in their careers that they are rewarded for good news—not bad news. When they become CEOs, they continue to focus on bringing good news to board members; then when really bad news is communicated, the board terminates the CEO. The best time to introduce bad news to the board is when there is some really good news and vice versa.

The late Bob Hampton, a former vice president at Witt Associates, Inc., stated that the selection of weak, non-threatening people in key management jobs is a primary cause of executive failure. He also echoes the findings of McCall and Lombardo, believing that poor "people skills" are a major cause.

Hampton believed that there is sometimes a failure of the board to define what they expect of the administrator. It is as though they are saying "If there is no problem, you are doing right; if there is a problem, we will get rid of you."

There are a number of danger signals or "yellow lights" executives should watch for. They include the following:

If there is a significant shift in the personnel to whom you report, you may be in trouble.

For example, you should be wary when a long-time board chairman retires from the board, and a new chairman with a different style and expectations takes office; a new CEO with a different management style arrives; or a number of significant changes occur at the senior management level. Any of these rapidly "shifting sands" can turn to "quicksand" for a healthcare executive who is not aware of their potential impact.

A "yellow light" should occur when your superiors hint that they are not pleased with some of the things that you have done or are doing. A comment such as, "We are a bit concerned," often means, "We think things are totally out of control." You also should see a warning signal when you no longer are invited to the meetings and activities in which you were once included.

A clear warning sign should appear when you find yourself increasingly disagreeing with others within the organization, including people other than your superiors or the medical staff.

You also should be wary if you have been passed over for a promotion and someone else has been brought in to fill the position. This does not necessarily mean that you will lose your job, or even that you will be encouraged to leave, but it does suggest that those who sit in judgment do not consider you to be worthy of a promotion at this time.

The probability of your derailment as a healthcare executive is somewhat proportional to the number of constituencies who can be marshaled against you. In other words, if the medical staff is unhappy with you, you are less apt to be terminated than if the medical staff, volunteers, employees, and public at large are dissatisfied with your work.

This phenomenon is not unique to the healthcare industry.

In the case of the resignation of a college president, first the faculty, then other unions, and, finally, even the students were calling for his resignation.

Medical staffs have learned that a "no confidence" vote may not terminate the targeted executive, but he or she will be "severely wounded" and the probability increases that the board or some other constituencies will join in the "hunt," eventually resulting in the executive's demise.

In another instance, the senior managers of a hospital complained bitterly to an outside consultant about a CEO and precipitated the CEO's termination after the consultant talked to the board.

Multiple "yellow lights" usually are the result of multiple mistakes in the executive's mode of intervention and innovation.

As stated previously, personality-related problems and power needs unfortunately compound an executive's problems. Many careers have been derailed over issues that should have been recognized and corrected by the executive involved long before they reached the danger level. It may be true that many healthcare executives are suffering, not because they cannot solve their problems, but because they cannot see their problems. As someone once said about their CEO, "Bill is ignorance on fire."

A logical question is, "Why do executives who are self-serving, self-centered, autocratic SOBs survive for so long—especially in senior level positions?" There are several reasons why it happens.

The first reason is that life is not fair. If you think it is fair, visit the pediatric wing in any tertiary medical center.

The second reason is that these individuals often come armed with opinions, while others shy away from effectively stating their convictions. I knew an executive at a Fortune 500 company whose major strength was his initiative and tactics of coming to any meeting (whether it was with two people or twenty) armed with opinions. They literally overwhelm others who come to meetings thinking meetings are "spectator sports."

The third reason is that they often achieve good short-term financial results. Shareholders like that, bond rating agencies like that, boards may like that, and senior management likes that. The cost in morale, long-term growth and especially turnover by talented personnel is often ignored or overlooked.

The good news (if there is any good news) about these types of bad managers is that when they are finally derailed, it often comes quickly. The autocratic executive who had been the CEO of a two-hospital system for eighteen years got into an argument with the board chairman one Friday. He was fired, and his office was cleaned out by Monday morning. There was "dancing in the streets" according to one senior vice president who was still there.

Chapter VII

Overcoming Failure

*"You can focus on your purpose
or you can focus on your problems,
but you cannot do both."*
—Reverend Rick Warren

Why devote a whole chapter to failure? There are several reasons. One reason is we all fail. If you haven't failed, and failed big, it is because you are early in your career. A second reason is that much of your success will come from how you bounce up off the bottom—not how you handle success.

Some consider losing one's job as synonymous with failure, and there are arguments that it may be true, while others argue that people often lose their positions through circumstances beyond their control. Regardless of the argument, because of the turnover of all the healthcare executives I have known in my career, my belief is that 85 percent of all health-care executives will be fired or forced to leave their position some time during their career.

The risk of being laid off increases as one gets older. The situation is compounded, because it also takes longer for older laid-off employees to find a new job. Moreover, once they do find a job, the older workers are more likely to take a bigger pay cut.

A study of workers from a cross section of industries, it revealed that the probability of being laid off between ages 44–45 was 7.5%. That percentage for workers age 55–59 is 10.3%, and 11.6% for workers age 60–64.[1] The average time needed to find a job is twenty-one weeks for someone age 35–44, and approximately twenty-five weeks for someone 45–55 years of age.[2]

Clearly, executives may sometimes be fired because of circumstances beyond their control. When that happens, one is reminded of the jingle about the good driver who died:

> He was right,
> Dead right, as he sped along.
> But he is just as dead
> As if he had been wrong.

Conversely, executives may retain their jobs until retirement, yet be considered failures because they misused their organizational power while in office and/or did not maximize the potential of either the organization or its staff.

One of the few studies of the mistakes that cause healthcare organizations to decline or even totally collapse suggests that errors in judgment by top management and boards (rather than external factors) are primary reasons for failing to maximize the potential within healthcare groups.   A quantitative study documenting the root causes of organizational decline in healthcare systems was done by the Health Care Advisory Board (HCAB 2002). All sixty organizations studied had experienced what the study calls a financial "flashpoint." An organization reaches a financial flashpoint when it experiences an overall five percentage point drop in margin in two years, a negative total margin, and has less than thirty days worth of cash on hand.

Of the factors studied leading to flashpoints, only 13 percent were uncontrollable. A full 87 percent could have been controlled, but weren't. The controllable factors were divided into two broad categories: strategic factors and organizational factors. Strategic factors included misperceptions about new business opportunities, overabundance of strategic initiatives and underestimation of acquisition demands, failure to exit underperforming strategies, and under investment in core business.

Of the controllable organizational factors cited in the study, the biggest cause for organizational decline was a culture of conservatism. Among the contributing factors were intolerance of dissent and an unwillingness to make unpopular decisions. Other organizational factors that helped bring the organizations studied to a financial flashpoint included inadequate performance measures, an overmatched management team, and lack of organizational accountability. Surprisingly, a cumbersome decision-making and board oversight process accounted for only three percent of the factors contributing to flashpoints.[3]

As Dr. Mark Silber has often stated, "Professionals are in a great horse race, a race between obsolescence and retirement. The best they can hope for is a photo finish."

There are a number of various degrees of failure, and some are related to the personal burnout of an individual. There are many individuals who never reach their full potential because of burnout. In this age of constant technological and professional breakthroughs, a person who fails to stay up-to-date cannot hope to advance. However, too many managers are quite satisfied with remaining where they are: their material needs are met; they become complacent, lulled into a false sense of security; and they see no need for improving their organization. If an organization has a large number of such individuals, particularly if they are in managerial positions, organizational failure is assured.[4] If you are such a person, remember what Henry Ford once said, "If you are coasting, you must be going downhill."

The levels of burnout shown in Exhibit 7-1[5] can occur long before someone loses her position.

Exhibit 7-1

"Degrees" of Personal Burnout

1st Degree Burnout	Failure to keep up-to-date
	Complacency
	Gradual loss of reality
2nd Degree Burnout	Accelerated physical deterioration
	• Loss of sleep
	• Loss of energy
	• Weight gain

Graduated indifference to work situation

3rd Degree Burnout	Major physical and/or
	psychological breakdown
	• Heart attack
	• Ulcer
	• Mental illness

Personal burnout can be a slow and subtle process—so slow that it is imperceptible to an executive. Friends and associates who will be honest with you about your actions are key to recognizing your need to make changes in your life. Cultivate close relationships with such people, and ask them to be open with you about your actions and how they are perceived.

For me, that kind of timely feedback has been provided for more than thirty-one years by my long-time assistant

(Peggy Lark) to whom this book is dedicated. On almost a daily basis, she has critiqued my written correspondence, my presentations, my actions, and me. Sometimes her comments have bordered on being brutal, but they have always been honest and have done more to keep me grounded than any other single factor or person in my career. If you have someone like that looking out for your welfare and covering your back, you are blessed. If you don't, you would do well to cultivate such a relationship with a colleague.

As noted previously, the executives interviewed all admitted to failing at something, but only one, Andy Andrews, admitted that he was forced to leave a position once in his career. The man he worked for apparently had an ego that was too big for the 221-bed hospital he oversaw in Phoenix. Subsequently, Andrew's boss bought a hospital in San Diego, and then he bought a county hospital in Florida. Andy said that one day the CEO called him in and said, "Andy, you'll only be happy if you have your own hospital." He went on to say "I still to this day do not know what happened. Psychologically, going through that was traumatic. I saw the guy about four years later, and my heart just kind of jumped, because it brought back all the bad memories which were devastating from a confidence level."

Making effective use of your time is one of the keys to any executive's survival. In their book, *Executive Stamina,*[6] authors Marty Geldman and Joshua Geldman have some suggestions for helping to assure that you take control of your calendar—both to thwart failure and to recover from it. Their suggestions include:

- Not spending time on low priority activities. List all your activities and prioritize them as high, medium, or low priority. Most of us "pass" a considerable amount of time doing things that have little tangible return.

- Not having a plan for your time. One of the most effective healthcare professionals I have ever known had daily lists, weekly goals, and long-range goals—all written down and all updated frequently. This subject will be described more in Chapter VIII.

- Limit interruptions. I once had a meeting with the number two executive of a Fortune 500 company—Hunter Henry. I was there to seek his advice. In the hour and forty-five minutes I met with him, his phone rang numerous times, but he never answered it. His assistant handled all the calls, but I am certain he responded to every call upon the conclusion of our conversation. In the years since that meeting, I have sought his advice numerous times, and he has always gotten back to me within twenty-four hours and usually the same day.

- Engaging with toxic people. These are the ones who

deplete and drain you. Some of these individuals are bullies; some just waste other's time in long conversations. Some are the opposite of mentors—they are "dementors"—a term not found in any dictionary. They spend their time correcting, controlling, and criticising others. Minimize your contact with them whenever possible. I have worked with "dementors" who survive, but drain hope and happiness from others in the organization.

- Wasting time in unproductive meetings. Meetings are the biggest time wasters of all, but meetings are the battlegrounds of business, and you must learn how to hold them and hold your own at them. Ask any chair how a meeting went, and they will probably say, "It was a good meeting. We got a lot done". However, with some frequency, if you ask some of the attendees at those same meetings how things went, they are apt to say, "I'll blow my brains out if I have to attend one more meeting like that."[7] If you chair a regular meeting, cancel it occasionally and try to objectively determine if there are any significant effects of not having it.

- Failing to overcome procrastination. There are three main reasons for procrastination.

The first reason is it may be a large project and may seem daunting. I have never written a book (including this one) without a delay of a couple of years from the time I conceptualize the topic and chapter outline. Much of the delay is caused by my own procrastination because of the time commitment such an effort requires. A second reason is it is a task that one is afraid of doing. It might be firing someone or some other situation that triggers avoidance behaviors. The third reason is tasks we don't like, e.g. number crunching, writing reports, going to your third fundraiser in a week, etcetera.

Move any of the above mentioned projects/tasks to the top of your "to do" list. Break big projects down into smaller units.

- Becoming addicted to technology. This is easy to do, and modern technology enables us to be available to almost anyone for anything and any time. Only you can tell if you are spending too much time online instead of face-to-face communications. Put your phone, Blackberry, etcetera. on vibrate, and don't answer it if you are in a meeting with one or more people.

- Unnecessary travel can drain you. I once gave a speech to eight people after traveling all day the previous day. It gave real meaning to the saying "a long run for a short slide." After every business trip

(whether it is long or short) reflect on whether or
not it was a good investment of your time.

One of the best books about coping with job loss and failure in general is *The Traveler's Gift* by Andy Andrews.[8] It is a fictional series of short stories about a man who has lost his job and meets a number of people from history—all who face challenges that made them famous. This type of book is often little more than a fairy tale, but *The Traveler's Gift* has seven lessons (decisions) one must make to overcome failure and be successful. It is a worthwhile read.

The first decision is **taking responsibility for the past**. The words, "It is not my fault" should never come out of someone's mouth.

The second decision for success is that the individual will **vow to seek wisdom**. They will choose their friends with care, and listen to the counsel of others while developing a servant's spirit.

The third decision for success one must make is to be **a person of action**. Leading is doing. As stated at the beginning of this chapter, all of us can focus on our problems, or we can focus on our purpose, but we cannot do both.

The fourth decision is to **have a decided heart**, which means you are passionate about your vision for the future. You are up early in the morning and are exhausted when you lay your head on your pillow at night.

The fifth decision is to **choose to be happy**. A key to assist with being happy is to smile at the people you meet, be grateful, be appreciative, and you are likely to find that you are happy.

The sixth decision a person should make is to **greet each day with a forgiving spirit**. To live your life according to the opinions of others is to be a slave.

The seventh and final decision one must make is that they will **persist without exception**. You must not be distracted. You know the outcome you desire. You stay the course and you do not quit—never, ever.

One final comment about failure from the General who many consider the greatest General of the 20th Century— George S. Patton, Jr.:

Life is not fair, and it never turns out exactly according to your plans. During a person's lifetime, there is no way to avoid problems, mishaps, and failure. Everyone experiences personal and professional setbacks, difficulties, and obstacles. These hindrances are unimportant, though, except as learning opportunities. What is important is how you react to them. If you want to feel sorry for yourself and give up, that is your prerogative. You always have the option to be a failure. If you want to be successful, however, accept these difficulties, learn from them, put your past behind you, and get on with your life and career. It takes personal strength of character and resilience to focus yourself and continue toward your objective in spite of the nasty little hurdles and barriers life puts in your pathway. If you really want something badly enough, nothing will stop you from getting it.[9]

Chapter VIII

Other Strategies
for Career Survival
and Success

*"The goodies in life do not come to those who labor.
The goodies in life come to those who labor and make
things happen—good things for your organization,
your friends, your family, and yourself."*

—Mark Silber, Ph.D.

To survive and advance in today's business environment requires that you fight on two fronts. The first, and perhaps most important, is your job. The second is your "other activities," that will help you prepare for your next career move, whether it is internally or externally.

In this regard, understand two things: 1) your career is not your job, and 2) most of your "other career activities" will be done on your so-called free time—and at your initiative.

Years ago, I had the opportunity to talk to a large number of university students at a convocation. I made the following analogy for them. I believe it also applies if you are in the work place. I know it applies to me.

I said that college is like a long train ride. You buy your ticket (pay your tuition) and you get on and ride. At the end of the semester, you get off the "train," and then you repeat the process the next semester. This process goes on for four years or more.

The mistake a number of college students make is they believe the train is taking them somewhere. The train isn't taking them anywhere. They are going to get off exactly where they got on. If it is the University of Texas, it is Austin. If it is the University of Florida, it is Gainesville. And, the only thing they are going to have to show for it are the skills they acquired while on the train ride.

If you are in the workplace, you have a similar situation. One day the "train" you are on will pull to a stop, and you will step off or get thrown off. The only thing you will have to show for it is the preparation you made for that eventuality. So, here are some suggestions about what you might do to prepare for that day:

- *Continue your education.* What a tragedy that many executives spend a concentrated period in academic study, and then focus only on the job at hand. There are numerous courses and seminars available to executives. It is almost frightening to see CEOs who haven't taken a formal course of any kind in years.

- *Participate in professional associations.* One of the best ways to meet other healthcare professionals is to participate actively in professional associations. Regional councils, state hospital associations, the American Hospital Association, and the American College of Healthcare Executives—all offer opportunities to meet others and hone your leadership skills.

- *Perfect your communication skills.* One way to do this is to write articles and books. The best piece of advice that can be given in this regard is to simply begin. It takes time, but it can be a worthwhile discipline, because it enables you to develop in-depth expertise in some field. In perfecting your speaking skills, the most important factor is practice. Teaching at a nearby college or university can be a great learning experience, and it looks good on a resume. If you cannot teach a course, at least seek professional speaking engagements.

- *Work at maintaining your health.* If healthcare executives could pursue only one activity in addition to their regular job duties, it should be maintaining their health. Being fit means being able to work, and healthcare executives must be fit enough to make it to retirement.

- *Maintain a job search folder.* Frequently, healthcare executives are terminated at a point when they do not have their resume updated or the materials at hand to construct one. It is important to maintain a folder at work or, preferably, at home, into which all information needed for your next search is placed. When you talk to someone who has lost their position, and two weeks later they say they are "working on their resume," you can bet they are ill-prepared.

- *Network.* It is easy for healthcare executives to become isolated. Even in a community with several hospitals, it is easy to be isolated because of the competitive nature of the healthcare industry. Therefore, it is wise to spend a portion of your time making professional contacts outside your facility. When you do, you should make a concentrated effort to work at meeting other healthcare professionals. Don't make the mistake of executives who treat seminars and other programs as on-the-job vacations, and therefore, do not take the time to get to know the other attendees.[1]

Preparing for your next job move requires a well-thought-out work plan, but more importantly, it requires discipline and perseverance. The most common refrain is, "But I do not have time." You have the same amount of time as all those who rise to the top. Everyone has the same 24 hours in their day and 365 days in their year. One thing is certain—when you are actively searching for a job, you will not have the luxury of time.

Perception is reality, and how your superiors perceive you is key to your advancement or derailment.

A fired chief executive officer stated that, in hindsight, he wished he had: 1) kept his superior better informed; 2) probed them as to what they were thinking, and 3) showed them that he was listening. That is advice that should be followed by anyone who works for an individual or group of individuals.

I have worked for one of the most outstanding healthcare leaders to ever walk the halls of a hospital (Ted Bowen, former president of The Methodist Hospital in Houston, Texas), and I have worked for a man who may have been the most autocratic healthcare executive in the United States. Regardless of the management style of your superiors, there are several fundamental "truths" to understand if you are to adequately serve and survive your superiors. Several of them are the same as those guidelines that were in Chapter V about working with boards. They are:

Your superior does not know what you are doing. You may think your superior knows what you are doing, and he or she may indicate that they know what you are doing, but they do not. They have too many issues of their own to be able to fully understand your areas of responsibility unless you effectively and continually communicate with them. Be sure that the information you give them is: 1) timely, 2) concise (use graphs whenever possible), and 3) do not make the mistake of only bringing good news—always mix good and bad news.

Your superior's priorities should be among your priorities. If your superior has a keen interest in a particular project or issue, then that issue should become a high priority of yours. It may be of minimal importance to the effectiveness of your particular organization or operations, but if it is a high priority to your superiors, then it should be something you vigorously address. Just as in working with boards, show your superiors you are listening by following up on their requests and suggestions.

You should know your superior(s) in-depth. You should know their expectations, their strengths, where they went to school, their family history, their friends, and who their heroes are. You should know what they are thinking about the organization, and you should constantly probe them to see if there is more that you could/should be doing. Are they receiving enough information about the right kind of subjects? A statement, "I'm a bit concerned" usually means "I think things are out of control."

Help solve his or her problems instead of asking them

to solve yours. Your superior has a number of pressures upon him or her—perhaps more than you have, and the more you can do to help them solve their problems, the better you will be perceived. Do not bring a problem without a recommended solution. It is a superior's responsibility to approve or disapprove your recommendation—not necessarily to recommend how your problem can be solved.

As will be discussed later in this chapter, this is particularly true if you have a new boss. New bosses aren't really interested in hearing about your problems. They have too many problems of their own. You may wish to talk to them about the issues/challenges you have before you, but do not present them with your problems and ask or expect them to solve your problems.

You will not change your superiors. Sometimes managers at any level question others about how they can change the person or group of people for whom they work. If your boss has a proclivity for conformance instead of performance or compliance instead of commitment, you are not going to change him or her. If she has a tendency to "major in minor issues," you will not change that either. If she has strong ego needs and enjoys taking credit for the successes of her subordinates, you will not change that or any other behavior. Do the best you can, and accommodate the individual's interests and quirks.

Several years ago, a friend and I finished giving a series

of presentations at the American College of Healthcare Executives, and one of the attendees came up afterward and talked about the person he worked for and all of his superior's bad traits, etcetera. The one-way conversation went on for what seemed like 10 minutes. When he finished, he said, "What can I do to change him?" My response was, "Nothing." I may have made my superiors (and I have had a great number of superiors by virtue of the numerous boards to which I have reported, as well as the CEOs I have worked for in my career), happy, sad, or mad, but I have never changed even one of them. This comes as bad news to many, but it is reality.

Lastly, observe those traits of your superiors you find rewarding and emulate them. Also, learn from your superior's traits that are frustrating and counter-productive. Be certain you are not guilty of developing similar patterns of behavior toward those who work for and with you.

When a new CEO enters, as happens often during most executive careers, the other executives should follow the advice in the previous paragraphs, but there are also some additional actions, that should be taken.

An informative study by Kevin Coyne and Edward Coyne, Sr.[2] outlines some of these recommended actions, and they have quantified the probability of senior executive turnover, depending on whether the new CEO is from within or from the outside. Based on the proxy statements of one thousand U.S. companies, they estimate the average turnover of senior executives in business is 17 percent (healthcare CEOs currently have about a 16 percent turnover rate as a national average). If there is a new CEO who is promoted from within, that turnover rate goes to approximately 22 percent. However, if a new CEO is brought in from outside, the turnover among senior executives jumps to 33 percent..

The authors say that most CEOs made their final determination about their management teams within sixty days of their arrival. Some of their suggestions for survival include:

Show your goodwill. Don't wait to let the new CEO know you want to be part of his or her management team. Do not assume the new CEO knows you want to cooperate. "If you decide you want to stay, let the CEO know, proactively, and without being sycophantic, that you want to be on the team, and follow up with actions that demonstrate your wiliness to go along with the program."[3]

Leave your baggage at the door. This includes a lot of don't. Don't talk about your compensation. Don't talk about your long-term plans. Don't raise issues about other executives. Don't forget to tell your spouse to be scrupulously polite. A spouse's comment can derail an executive as quickly as a comment made by the executive.

Understand the CEO's agenda. It is not enough to just understand the new CEO's agenda. You should confirm with the new CEO that you understand what the priorities are.

Be on your "A" game. Forget about taking a vacation.

Come to meetings (all meetings) prepared, and listen to everything the new CEO says. As I once heard a very successful corporate raider say, "This isn't summer camp—we are here to compete." Be ready to take the "playing field," and play his or her "game."

The bottom line is, "Make your personal decision about whether the new group style, vision, and business practices are ones you want to live with. Then commit or get out. Otherwise, everyone's life will be hell. And the result will be the same anyway."[4]

Chapter IX

Concluding Thoughts

"There is no longer any corporate career ladder.
There isn't even a rope ladder. It is more like jungle vines
and you bring your own machete."
—Peter Drucker,
Chicago Sun Times, November 21, 1993

Some final thoughts for healthcare executives and others that are not covered in the previous chapters.

Great executives are choreographers. It has been said that a good gunfighter is so fast, you *can barely see* his hand move. However, a great gunfighter is so fast, you *do not see* his hand move. Great executives don't "bang the drum," talking about themselves and/or spend a lot of time making clichéd statements such as, "We are playing to win"; "We have to work smarter, not harder," etcetera.

Great executives work harder than others choreographing

what they want to have happen. They work with all the key stakeholders on the board, medical staff, volunteers, and community members to accomplish the goals of the organization and maximize its potential.

Nowhere is this more evident than in meetings. The greatest executives I have known don't have to say very much in a meeting because they have choreographed what they want to occur. For them, it is like watching a movie they have directed, knowing that they have already seen the ending.

Character is Key

One of the traits I noted about everyone who contributed to this book was they had excellent character. I knew that when I selected them, but everything they said and have done confirmed that these professionals have great character.

In a graduation address in 2006, Lawrence Reed, former president of the Mackinac Center for Public Policy, addresses what he states is, "More important than all the good grades you have earned, more important than all the college degrees you'll accumulate, and, indeed, more important than all the knowledge you'll ever absorb in your lifetimes. It's something over which every responsible thinking adult has total personal control, and yet millions of people every year sacrifice it for very littlie. It will not only define and shape your future; it will put both a concrete floor under it and an iron ceiling over it. It is what the world will remember you for more than probably anything else. It's not your looks, it's not your talents, it's not your ethnicity and, ultimately, it may not even be anything you ever say. This incredibly powerful thing is "character."[1]

Reed goes on to tell the story of something that happened in the little town of Conyers, Georgia, in the mid 1980s. "When school officials there discovered that one of their basketball players who had played 45 seconds in the first of the school's five post-season games, and actually been scholastically ineligible, they returned the state championship trophy the team had just won a few weeks before. If they had simply kept quiet, probably no one else would have ever known about it, and they could have retained the trophy.

To their eternal credit, the team and the town, dejected though they were, rallied behind the school's decision. The coach said, "We didn't know he was ineligible at the time—but you have got to do what is honest and right, and that is what the rules say. I told my team that people forget the scores of the games; they don't ever forget what you're made of."[2]

Doing the "right thing" was echoed by General Norman Schwarzkopf at a luncheon in Detroit several years ago. I attended, thinking he would talk about his experiences in Desert Storm—a battle that military strategists will talk about for a thousand years. Or, I thought that he might talk about what he had learned as a cadet at West Point, or the heroics that earned him a Silver Star in Viet Nam.

Instead, he talked about none of those events. What he did talk about was an experience when he arrived at the Pentagon as a Two Star General. He wanted a briefing with the Three Star General he was replacing. As he watched the Three Star General and the General's aide "pack up" their office, he said, "I need some advice as to what to do." The Three Star General said, "Just Follow Rule 12." Schwarzkopf said, "What is Rule 12?" The response was, "When in charge, take charge."

Schwarzkopf said he literally followed the Three Star General down the hall asking him questions. Finally, the Three Star General said, "Just follow rule 13." "And what is that?" Schwarzkopf asked. "When in charge, do the right thing," was the response. So there, in a 'nutshell,' was Schwarzkopf's advice—"When in charge, take charge"—and "When in charge, do the right thing." That is sage advice for any leader.

In an article about managing yourself, Robert Kaplan emphasizes the need to demonstrate character in leadership. He states, "While seemingly amorphous, character and leadership often make the difference between good performance and great performance. One measure of character is the degree to which you put the interests of your company and colleagues ahead of your own. Excellent leaders are willing to do things for others without regard to what's in it for them. They coach and mentor. They have the mindset of an owner and figure out what they would do if they were the ultimate decision maker. They're willing to make a recommendation that would benefit the organization's overall performance, possibly to the detriment of their own unit. They have the courage to trust that they will eventually be rewarded, even if their actions may not be in their own short-term interest."[3]

Jack Krasula is a talk show host in Detroit and has interviewed famous people and peak performers for years. He provides an insight into what made them successful leaders. He states, "As I reflect on the common traits of the 90-plus guests, I came up with the following:[4]

- They started with nothing but a huge dream against insurmountable odds.
- Each one had life give them huge setbacks, curve-balls, etcetera.
- They held on when most would have quit.
- They did their best each day.
- They believe in serving others.
- They surround themselves with great people who had the same culture and were world-class in the role they played.
- They set extremely high standards for themselves and their team.
- They are masters at communication.
- They are optimists.
- They have stayed humble.
- They give back to their fellow man each day.

- They view each day as a new tryout.
- Faith has played a role in their lives.

Lastly, he said that often the greatest setback, the most unbelievable life-changing event turned out to be the "greatest thing that has ever happened" in their lives. Hopefully, the setbacks we all experience will empower us—not imprison us.

One final comment: Healthcare professionals would do well to not let others define them. My observation is that the majority of people treat others as *less than they really are*. At best, an even smaller group of people treat others pretty much *as they are*. We all have frailties and failures, and this second group is quick to point them out to us and to others when they are talking about us. Is it any wonder most of us never maximize our potential?

Set high standards for yourself and work tirelessly to rise above the naysayer. Assure that your tomorrows are better than today. Your best days are either ahead of you or behind you. If you are a "learner," I'm betting your best days are ahead of you.

Contributors

Andrew Allen is a former president of Carondelet Health System—a national Catholic healthcare system of sixteen acute hospitals. He has also held a number of other CEO positions throughout the U.S.A. He received his MPH from Tulane University.

Sandra Bennett Bruce is president of St. Alphonsus Regional Medical Center, Boise, Idaho—a 345-bed regional referral center. It also owns St. Benedict's Hospital, a 40-bed, long-term care hospital, and manages two other hospitals. She has held CEO positions for almost thirty years. She received a master's degree in health administration from the University of Notre Dame.

Jerry Fitzgerald is the immediate past president of Oakwood Healthcare, Inc., a multi-hospital system located in Detroit, Michigan, where he served as CEO for three decades.

He has served as chair of the AHA Regional Policy Board, twice as chair of the Michigan Hospital Association, and other professional organizations too numerous to mention. He received his master's degree in hospital administration from the University of Michigan.

Doug Peters is former president and CEO of the Jefferson Health System in Philadelphia. He has served in executive positions with Blue Cross and Blue Shield, Henry Ford Health System, and the University of Nebraska Medical Center. He holds a master's degree in hospital administration from the University of Michigan.

John Rockwood is immediate past president of Munson Healthcare System in Traverse City, Michigan, which owns three medical centers and manages three others. He has a strong financial background and has held numerous leadership positions in his professional societies. He received his master's degree in business administration from Boston University.

Mark Taylor is president of Genesys Regional Health System in Grand Blanc, Michigan—a 410-bed facility with a number of other affiliates. Prior to that, he was president of St. John's Medical Center in Detroit. He holds a master's degree in health services administration from The University of Michigan. He has a breadth of experience in healthcare—especially in various aspects of human resource management.

Samuel Wallace is immediate past president of the Iowa Health System. At the time he retired, Iowa Health System was comprised of 23 hospitals, 500+ physicians, several nursing homes, a multi-state home health agency, and two schools of higher education. He was a governor in the ACHE and a fellow classmate of mine at Washington University in St. Louis, Missouri, where he received his master's degree in hospital administration.

Gail Warden is immediate past president of Henry Ford Health Care System. He has held several other CEO positions in large hospitals in various parts of the United States. He also served as CEO of a large HMO in Washington. He is a prolific author and speaker, and is a nationally recognized healthcare leader having served as chair of the board of the American Hospital Association. He has received the "Gold Medal" from both the AHA and ACHE. He received his master's degree in hospital administration from the University of Michigan.

Notes

I. Experiences That Shaped Us

1.   Jon Katzenbach and Jason Santamaria. "Firing Up the Front Line,"
      Harvard Business Review, May/June, 1999, p. 112.

II. If I Knew Then What I Know Now

1.   Keith Ferrazzi, *Never Eat Alone: And Other Secrets to Success, One
      Relationship at a Time*, (Doubleday, New York, NY, 2005), p. 87

2.   The Best Advice I Ever Got," *Fortune*, May 12, 2008, p. 74.

3.   Terence F. Moore and Earl A. Simendinger, Ph.D., *Turnarounds: Lessons in
      Leadership*, Health Administration Press, Ann Arbor, MI, 1993.

4.   Richard Edler, *If I Knew Then What I Know Now*, (Berkley, New York, NY,
      1995), pp. 120–122.

5.   Anne Fisher, "What is the One Piece of Advice You Wish You Had Been
      Given," *Fortune*, June 23, 2003, p. 142).

6.   Terence F. Moore, *Power: Its Use and Abuse*, 1997 (ISBN 0-9633518-6-9).

7.   Tom Peters, "Power: The Pursuit of Wow," *Success*, November 1994. p. 33.

8.   Ibid, p. 34.

III. Working With the Management Team

1.   Steve Chandler and Duane Block, *The Hands-Off Manager*, Career Press,
      2007, p. 20

2.   Ibid, p. 20.

3.   Terence F. Moore and Earl A. Simendinger, Ph.D., *Hospital Turnarounds:
      Lessons in Leadership*, Beard Books, 1999, p. 213.

4.   J. Gabarro, *The Dynamics of Taking Charge*, Harvard Business School
      Press, 1985, p. 51.

5.   Larry Winget, *It's Called Work For A Reason*, Gotham Books, New York,
      NY, 2007, p. 129.

6.   Ibid, p. 130.

7.   Ibid, p. 131.

8.   William Taylor, "The Leader of the Future: Interview with Ron Heifetz,"
      Fast Company, June 1999, p. 130–138.

9.   Warren Bennis, Ph.D., "The End of Leadership: Exemplary Leadership
      Is Impossible Without Full Inclusion, Initiatives, and Cooperation
      of Followers,, *Organizational Dynamics*, V 28, No. 1, Summer 1999,
      pp.71–79.

IV. Working With the Medical Staff

1.   "How to Involve (The Right) Physicians in the Leadership Process,"
      Hospital Forum, May/June 1985, p. 61.

2.   Ibid, p. 62.

3.   Earl A. Simendinger, Ph.D. and Terence F. Moore, "The Formation and
      Destruction of Physician-Administrator Cooperation," *Michigan Hospitals,*
      April, 1986, p. 26.

4.   Earl A. Simendinger, "The Formation and Destruction of Administrator-
      Physician Cooperation," unpublished Ph.D. Dissertation, Case Western
      Reserve.

5.   Kaplan, "Open Interaction: Form, Function and Feasibility," *Advances
      in Experimental Social Processes,* Vol. 1, edited by Cary L. Cooper and
      Clayton R. Adderfer, New York: Chichester, 1978.

6.   Joseph Bujak, M.D., A presentation to the Michigan Hospital Association's
      Governance Institute, Mt. Pleasant, Michigan, April 27, 2009.

7.   Richard Thompson, M.D., "Some Keys to Working with Physicians,"
      Trustee, November 1979, pp 33–34.

8.   Terence F. Moore and Earl A. Simendinger, Ph.D., "Involving the Right
      Physicians," *Michigan Hospitals,* May 1990, p. 46.

9.   Jeff Goldsmith, "Driving the Nitroglycerin Truck," *Healthcare Forum,*
      March/April 1993, p. 37.

10.   "Disruptive Physicians: Enough is Enough," *The Credentialing Institute,*
      1993, pp. 1–4.

V. Optimizing Boards and Board Relationships

1.   Terence F. Moore and Mark Silber, Ph.D., "Optimizing Board/CEO
      Relationships," *Michigan Hospitals* May/June 1992.

VI. Mistakes Managers Make

1.   David Brown, "Fast Trackers Can Lack Ethics, Vision," *Canadian HP
      Reporter* 16: 8–11 (online) retrieval http://www.ref.oclc.org.

2.   A. Vogl, "Understanding Failure", *Across Board* 40, pp. 27–32.

3.   Michael M. Lombardo and Morgan W. McCall, "*Issues and Observations,"*
      February 1983, Vol. 3, Issue 1, pp. 1-4.

4.   Michael M. Lombardo and Morgan W. McCall, "What Makes a Top
      Executive," *Psychology Today,* February 1983, Vol. 17, issue 2, pp. 26–31.

5.   Terence F. Moore and Earl A. Simendinger, Ph.D., "Executive Failure,"
      Healthcare Forum, May/June, 1987. pp. 61–64.

6.   Lombardo and McCall, p. 28.

VII. Overcoming Failure

1.   Paul Keegan, *Laid off at 50, Money,* January 2009, p. 86.

2.   Ibid.

3.   Terence F. Moore and David Zuza, "Strategic Misjudgments: Lessons
      Learned," Spectrum, September/October 2007, p. 4.

4.   John J. McCarthy, *Why Managers Fail,* McGraw-Hill, New York, 1978; p.
      209.

5.   Earl A. Simendinger and Terence F. Moore, *Organizational Burnout in Healthcare Facilities: Strategies for Prevention and Change*, Aspen Publication, Rockville, Maryland, 1985, p. 55.

6.   Marty Geldman, Ph.D. and Joshua Geldman, *Executive Stamina: How to Optimize Time, Energy and Productivity to Achieve Peak Performance*, John Wiley and Sons, Inc., Hoboken, New Jersey, 2008.

7.   Terence F. Moore, *Administrative Warfare*, Chapter 7 (Meetings are the Battlegrounds of Business), 2007 (ISBN 0-9633518-5-0).

8.   Andy Andrews, *The Traveler's Gift*, Nelson Books, Nashville, TN, 2002.

9.   Charles M. Province, *Patton's One-Minute Messages*, Presidio Press, Navoto, California, 1995, p. 76.

VIII. Other Strategies for Career Survival and Success

1.   Terence F. Moore "What to Do Between Job Searches," *Michigan Hospitals*, May 1991, page 43.

2.   Kevin Coyne and Edward Coyne, Sr., "Surviving Your New CEO," *Harvard Business Review*, May 2007, pages 62–69.

3.   Ibid, page 66.

4.   Ibid, page 64.

IX. Concluding Thoughts

1.   Lawrence Reed, *The Difference One Can Make: The Importance of Character*, Commencement Address, Thomas Jefferson Independent Day School, Joplin, Missouri, May 21, 2006.

2.   Ibid, p. 9.

3.   Robert Kaplan, "Reaching Your Potential," *Harvard Business Review*, July/August 2008, p. 47.

4.   Jack Krasula, "Thoughts on Success: Advice From Those Who Have Been There," *Corp.*, March 2007, Vol. 10, #2, p. 12.